Our Little Secret

S.L. STERLING

Our Little Secret
© 2022 S.L. Sterling

Our Little Secret

Copyright © 2022 by S.L. Sterling

All rights reserved. Without limiting the rights under copyright reserved about, no part of this publication may be reproduced, stored in, or introduced into a retrieval system, or transmitted in any form or by any means (mechanical, electronic, photocopying, recording, or otherwise) without the prior written permission of both the copyright owner and the above publisher of the book. This is a work of fiction. Any references to historical events, real people, or real places are used fictitiously. Other names, characters, places, and events are products of the author's imagination, and any resemblance to actual events or places or persons, living or dead, is entirely coincidental. Disclaimer: This book contains mature content not suitable for those under the age of 18. It involves strong language and sexual situations. All parties portrayed in sexual situations are consenting adults over the age of 18.

ISBN: 978-1-989566-20-6

Paperback ISBN: 978-1-989566-32-9

Editor: Brandi Aquino, Editing Done Write

Cover Design: Thunderstruck Cover Design

Ainsley

I stared out of my bedroom window down into my next-door neighbor's backyard and watched as he walked behind his mower, cutting his lawn. I looked forward to every Saturday morning, because that was the day that Spencer would appear shirtless and do all his yard work. Spencer and his little girl, Nikki, had moved in almost a year ago now, and from the time I'd laid eyes on him, I'd wanted him. Problem was, he was a good twenty years older, divorced, and a father, and I had only turned twenty a few months ago. Not that any of that mattered, except for the fact that he was also my father's best friend.

"Still staring at your god?" Carly questioned.

"How did you guess?"

"Well, you were actually in mid-sentence, and you just stopped talking." Carly giggled. "That was the only logical reason I could come up with. Unless, of course, you were having a stroke."

I rolled my eyes. "I'm sorry, but how is it even possible that he can look just as sexy in grubby sweats, covered in sweat, as he does every weekday morning when he leaves for the office dressed to the nines in a suit and tie?" I questioned. "I mean, it doesn't help that the man is beautiful. Thick, dark hair I'd love to run my fingers through, blue eyes anyone with half a pulse could get lost in, 6'2" and a solid wall of pure muscle that I'd love to lay under. God, how I'd love to lay under him." I grew quiet envisioning that image. "But in all seriousness, he looks dynamite dressed in a suit, and he looks just as amazing now."

"God, I know what the man looks like, Ainsley. His picture is plastered on every bus stop and major billboard all over the damn city." She sighed with irritation. The topic of Spencer Brooks had dominated every conversation we'd had for the past year.

"I think he makes the city look better. You can't honestly tell me that you don't agree?"

The phone was silent for a moment, and then I heard a huge sigh. "Is Spencer Brooks all we are going to talk about today?"

"I'm sorry...it's just..."

"It's just you're obsessed with an older man," Carly bit out. "One who just happens to be the same age as your father, which is just gross. He's also, in case you've forgotten, your soon-to-be boss! Did you forget about that? It's seriously quite a predicament you've gotten yourself into."

I glanced out the window again, hoping to catch a glimpse of Spencer one more time, but he had disappeared, leaving the lawn mower in the middle of the yard. I frowned as I did a quick search around the back yard but couldn't see him anywhere.

"Well, it's my predicament isn't it," I mumbled.

"You know, girl, I was thinking, Craig really likes you. Perhaps you should go for him. He will be there with us tonight. That is, if you are coming," Carly said.

"I'm...I'm not sure if I am going just yet," I mumbled, distracted by a voice coming from downstairs. I could hear my father speaking with someone and I strained to hear who it was.

"Come on, how do you not know yet? It's Jon's birthday. He is really looking forward to partying, and I don't think I need to remind you that you did, in fact, promise him you would be there the other day when we had coffee together! You can't back out now."

I heard a rumble of laughter from downstairs, followed by our neighbor's deep voice. A surge of excitement ran through me.

"How about I call you back in five. He's here," I sighed into the phone.

"Who's there? Ainsley, come on. I'm trying to get final numbers for reservations, that is why I called you over a half hour ago, not to talk about Spencer. I just need to know if you are in or out."

"The one, the only, Spencer Brooks," I whispered, ignoring what she had asked me. I heard Carly groan her displeasure into the phone as I opened my bedroom door a little farther just to catch the sound of his deep, sexy voice. I was sure she was tired of listening to me go on and on about Spencer, but I couldn't help myself.

"Girl, you've got it bad. Seriously, I think you should go for Craig. If not him then perhaps someone at school has turned your head."

"The guys at school are dull," I whined. "None of them are mature like Spencer." Another burst of laughter came from downstairs, catching my attention, followed by his deep, sexy voice that gave me chills.

"Spencer should be mature he owns his own company and has a daughter."

"I'll call you back in ten minutes. Oh, and Craig isn't my type," I said.

"Ainsley, he's the captain of your university football team. How the hell is that not your type? He's almost six feet, with dark hair and blue eyes and what was it...a wall of pure muscle." Carly giggled. "Sounds exactly like a younger Spencer."

"You are impossible. I'll call you back."

"Oh, Ains...come on. I just need a yes or no. The reservations—"

"Got to go," I whispered, cutting her off and hanging up the phone. I wandered over to my dresser, checking out my reflection in the mirror and fluffing my hair. I pulled my bulky sweatshirt over my head and smiled as I looked at myself in my fitted tank top and jean shorts. That's much better, I thought to myself. I grabbed my glass from my desk, opened my bedroom door, and headed down toward the kitchen.

I stopped in the hallway just outside the kitchen door and took a deep breath. I needed to gather myself before I walked into that kitchen.

"Spencer, what you really need is a hot twenty-year-old to fuck the shit out of," I heard my father say.

Immediately, at my father's words, I imagined Spencer placing me up against a wall and having his way with me. My body heated at the very thought. I was twenty and I would more than happily allow him to have his way with me, I thought to myself. I took a deep breath, pulled my tank top down, then took a step forward.

"That will help you get Brittany out of your system," my father said as I rounded the corner.

Almost instantly, I met Spencer's blue eyes. I swallowed hard as I saw them quickly roam over my body before they came back up to my face. I looked down at his large, muscular hands, instantly wondering what they would feel like as they gripped my hips. I swallowed hard, smiled, and did my best to keep the heat from rising to my face.

"Good morning, Ainsley," Spencer said, clearing his throat, his eyes skimming over my chest again. "Any plans for tonight?"

"Hey, Ains!" Dad said, taking a sip of his beer.

"Hey, Dad. Hey, Mr. Brooks. No, not yet. Carly wants me to go out," I replied as I reached for the orange juice in the fridge and poured myself a glass, then turned and leaned against the counter.

"Ahhh to be young again." My father chuckled.

"Ainsley, I told you, call me Spencer. This Mr. Brooks nonsense can stop. It will just be a formality when you start at the office." He winked, picking up his beer and taking a swig.

I was going to be interning at his office over the summer as his executive assistant, while his regular assistant was off on medical leave. "Of course, Spencer," I replied. His name felt thick on my tongue, and as I looked at him, his eyes once again roamed over my body.

"Oh gosh, excuse me for a minute. I'll get that drill you wanted to borrow, Spencer," Dad said, getting up off his chair and leaving the two of us alone together in the room.

The air suddenly felt thick as Spencer's eyes met mine. My eyes burned as the nervous flutter in my stomach began again. The longer we stared at one another, the more the heat grew within me and the more intense it became. I was glad when a loud ring finally pulled his eyes from mine and he began checking something on his cell phone that sat on the table in front of him.

While he was reading, I couldn't help but let my eyes roam over his muscular arms and broad, strong chest and shoulders. I was completely lost in thought as to what he must feel like when he cleared his throat and my eyes flashed to his face. I had no idea how long he had been watching me watch him, but the smirk he wore told me it had been long enough. I wanted to die. How embarrassing. I could feel the heat in my cheeks as I met his eyes.

"Here it is!" Dad said, coming back into the kitchen and placing the drill on the counter. He was completely oblivious to the way Spencer looked at me.

I cleared my throat and reached for something in the cupboard so my father couldn't see my flushed cheeks. As I let out a breath and turned back to them, my father sat back down, grabbed his beer, and took a swig, and then began talking with Spencer again as if I weren't even in the room.

I slowly faded out of the conversation as I watched Spencer grip the neck of his beer bottle, bring it to his lips, and tip his head back, emptying the bottle's contents. I couldn't help but watch the taught muscles in his throat as he swallowed. Then my eyes traveled to his large, muscular hands once again. *God he hand nice hands.* A pulse of excitement ran through me as I wondered what it would feel like if they were on my body, touching me in places that I'd only ever imagined being touched in. *Carly was right, this had to stop. There was no way I could spend my summer in this state, nor be like this while I worked under him, I mean beside him.* Spencer placed the bottle on the table and his eyes wandered back over to me, and then he flashed that sexy smirk in my direction.

"Oh, Ainsley, before I forget, do you think you could watch Nikki for Spencer on the twelfth next month?"

I looked to my father and then over to Spencer who waited for my reply.

"I have that Valentine's Day function I'm hosting for my clients, and it's my weekend to have her," Spencer replied.

Nikki was Spencer's three-year-old daughter. He shared custody of her after he and his wife separated a year ago. When Spencer had Nikki, I usually always babysat for her when he had a work function.

"Yep, sure thing. I'd better go call Carly back." I pushed myself off the counter and left the kitchen, turning quickly to look back at Spencer one last time. I noticed his gaze was firmly planted on my ass, and he quickly averted his eyes as soon as he knew I had caught him. I waited one second, and as his eyes met mine, I smiled at him over my shoulder and continued down the hall, stopping halfway once again to listen to their conversation.

"So, like I said before Ains came in, you need a hot twenty-year-old to fuck her from your mind."

"Where the hell am I going to find that? I'm over the hill. Besides, I'm over Brittany, I just think I'm having a hard time with the loneliness."

I swallowed hard as I listened. One thing Spencer Brooks was not was over the hill.

"Surely you could find a girl at one of these functions of yours," my father responded.

"No, I don't think so. However, you should come with me to this function on the twelfth, that way you can see what my company can do for you," he said to my father.

"You want me to go, but tell me this, why don't you use your own company to find your twenty-year-old then if it's so great?"

"My company isn't for hookups. It's for long-term, meaningful relationships, which is something I'm not sure I'm looking for right now. It's been a hard year for me. I think I just want to have some fun, you know, no strings."

"I understand. I remember how it was for me after Ain's mom left. However, like you, I don't know what I want." I heard my father say, "I'm not sure I want to get involved with someone long term. I've barely dated since Ainsley's mother left."

"I totally understand, but you won't know until you try something. I'll send you over a trial pass, that way you can look around, and if you don't like what you see, no hard feelings. I'll send over a couple extras for some of your friends at work too."

"Sounds good, Spencer. I've got to get going. It's grocery day. I also have errands to run in the city."

"Okay, see you later then. I'll drop off those passes later this afternoon. I'll leave them in the mailbox if you aren't home."

"I look forward to it."

I listened as the chairs scraped across the floor and went back into my room, shutting the door.

Ainsley

A trial for my father. I let out a breath, not sure if I was ready for him to start dating. I leaned against the cool door, trying to cool myself off. I grabbed my phone and dialed Carly's number. While waiting for her to answer, I grabbed the magazine I had purchased, flopped down on my bed, and began flipping through the pages.

"It's about time you called me back. What the hell took so long?"

"Yeah, sorry about that," I said, continuing to flip through the pages. "Spencer asked me to babysit."

"Tonight?"

"No, not tonight," I bit out as I slowly flipped the page.

"So then you are coming with us tonight right?"

I flipped to the next page and instantly all the air left the room. In front of me was an ad for *Finding Forever* with Spencer on it. He sat at a table, a coffee in front of him, looking into the camera, those blue eyes of his sparkling. Spencer Brooks owned *Finding Forever*; it was one of the top, elite matchmaking companies in the world, and I would soon be working side-by-side with that hunk of a man. "Holy shit!" I exclaimed.

"What?" Carly asked with excitement.

"You're never going to believe this. Do you have the new *Cosmo* mag that came out last week?" I questioned, looking over the ad and all the manly goodness that was Spencer in the photo.

"Yeah, I think so, why?"

"Get it and look at page twenty-five."

"Ainsley, really, I just need to know if you are coming tonight. Seriously, babe, I need to get the reservations placed. The place fills up so fast, and if I don't, my head will be on the chopping block."

"Get the magazine!" I gritted out between clenched teeth. "Page twenty-five."

I studied the page, and that was when I noticed in small letters, in the upper right-hand corner of the page, what appeared to be an ID handle for his dating site.

"What am I supposed to be looking for?" Carly huffed.

"My God, just go to page twenty-five. You'll see." I

could hear Carly frantically flipping through the pages, and finally she stopped.

"Yeah, so, it's your Greek god, so what."

"Look up in the corner. Looks like it could be his ID handle, RomanticAlpha42."

"Oh, Ainsley!! You're crazy. As if the man is going to post his real handle to the world. Get a freaking grip. Now are you coming with us tonight or not?"

I slid off my bed and wandered over to my desk and opened my laptop, quickly typing in *Finding Forever* in the search bar. Within seconds, the page had loaded. "Um, sure, I guess."

"All right got to go. Oh, and, Ains, don't do anything stupid, okay."

"What is that supposed to mean?"

"Exactly what I said. Don't do anything stupid. Promise me."

I rolled my eyes. "I thought you had to place the reservation?"

"I do, just don't do anything stupid."

"Go call," I said and hung up the phone, burying my face back into the computer.

I turned my attention to the website. I'd been meaning to check it out for a while, especially after I'd been hired. I read through the FAQ page and noticed they offered a free two-week trial. I bit my bottom lip as Carly's words floated through my mind not to do anything stupid. I looked over at the magazine sitting beside me, staring at his handle. *Could it really be his?*

Two weeks, that would be all I would need to find out if it was really him, I thought to myself. I could sign up, contact him, and I wouldn't mention a single word to Carly about it. It would be my secret.

I clicked on "signup" and began setting up my profile, quickly creating a username, and hit next. My stomach sank when the next screen loaded. They wanted credit card information.

"Fuck," I muttered under my breath. I nervously tapped my finger on the mouse, trying to decide what I should do. Then I closed the laptop, there was no way I could give my credit card information to the company. What if Spencer had access to that information.

I got up off my chair and ran my fingers through my hair, feeling completely unsettled. I flipped my stereo on, one of my favorite songs blaring through the speakers, then turned around to see the magazine open to the advertisement. I pulled it closer, studying the handle once again, then looked to my laptop. I blew out a frustrated sigh and then grabbed my purse. "What could it hurt? I'll just make sure I cancel before the free trial period is over," I mumbled, curiosity getting the best of me.

I sat back down at my desk and opened my laptop again and typed in my credit card details. A few more clicks and I was in, staring at a bunch of questions that needed to be answered before they would let me start searching. I used most of my real facts that way I wouldn't have to remember any lies, and forty-five minutes later, BabyGirl89 had been born.

I hit search and typed in RomanticAlpha42, and within seconds, I was faced with a picture-less profile. My stomach churned with excitement that I could barely contain, as I read over the profile, which barely contained anything that would lead me to believe this was Spencer.

I hovered my mouse over the contact button, my stomach flopping with nerves. What if it wasn't him? My hand shook at the thought. I sat there staring at the screen, almost sure I was going to be sick. I grabbed my phone and dialed Carly.

"Let me guess, you've changed your mind and you aren't coming with us after all."

"No, I'll be there. But you won't believe this, but it was real."

"What was real? Ainsley, what are you talking about?"

"RomanticAlpha42."

"Ainsley!"

"What?"

"Tell me you didn't sign up. Tell me you didn't send a message to that profile."

I was quiet as I listened to my friend panic on the

other end of the phone. "Ainsley, please tell me you didn't."

"I haven't messaged it. Not yet anyways. But I did create myself a profile," I said as I hit the connect button below RomanticAlpha's name and began typing.

"Oh, Ainsley, do not message that profile. It could be anybody. Besides, you need to get ready for dinner. I'll be picking you up in an hour."

"Too late!"

"Too late? What do you mean too late?"

"I just sent my first connection email!" I giggled into the phone.

"What???" Girl, you are impossible, and you are going to get yourself into trouble."

"I know and I know, but that is why you love me."

I grabbed my purse and followed Carly out to the car. Tonight, had been fun, until Craig had shown up. He'd slid into the booth beside me and hadn't let me move. The only reprieve I'd gotten was when he had headed to the men's room.

"I can take Ainsley home if you like, Carly," Craig called, as he and Jon hurried to catch up to us.

"It's okay, Carly has to get something from my house that she forgot the other day," I lied.

"Oh, what did I forget?" Carly said, looking at me with confusion.

All three of them looked at me as I struggled to come up with something that Carly had forgotten. "You know...that thing," I bit out, meeting her eyes.

"Ainsley, I'm sure I haven't forgotten anything."

"Yes, you did. Remember, I told you earlier," I said, grabbing her arm and whispering in her ear to just go along with it.

"Oh, that's right. I know what it is."

Jon and Craig both looked at us as we approached Carly's car. I went around to the passenger's side and waited for Carly to open the door when Craig came up beside me.

"How about I call you tomorrow? Perhaps we could go out to a movie or something."

I nodded. "Sure, if you like." I smiled, looking in Carly's direction. "Can you unlock the door."

"Talk to you tomorrow," Craig said as he leaned in and placed a kiss on my cheek just as the locks on the door opened.

I climbed into the front seat and pulled my phone from my pocket. I'd promised Carly I wouldn't check it at dinner tonight, but as soon as I checked my email, I'd wished I'd stayed home.

Carly climbed in the front seat beside me and shoved the key into the ignition, turning the car on. She adjusted the radio and put on her seatbelt, while I sat there staring at my screen.

"Well, that went well. See, I told you Craig likes you. You really need to give him a chance. Oh, and the next time you want to use me for a lie, just tell me ahead of time okay."

"Um..."

"Um what? What are you looking at? Did Craig message you already? Is there love in the air between you two?"

I sat there staring down at my phone, at the email I'd received almost one hour after I'd left the house.

"Ainsley, what is it?" Carly asked, her voice full of concern.

I looked at her, a smile creeping onto my face, and slowly turned my phone for her to see. RomanticAlpha42 had responded to my contact email. I swallowed hard as she read his words.

"What are you going to do about that?" she questioned, looking from the screen then up to me.

"What do you think I'm going to do? I'm going to respond to him," I said. "Now what should I say." I pulled my phone back and hit reply.

"Honestly? I think you should leave it alone, Ainsley.

You're playing with fire," Carly said as she put the car in reverse and backed out of the parking spot.

I read the response from him one more time as Carly's words floated through my mind. I blew out a breath, shut the phone off, and shoved it into my purse. I'd sleep on it, and if I still felt I needed to respond in the morning I would, but for now, I was going to follow her advice.

Ainsley

RomanticAlpha42: I'd love to bury my face between those creamy thighs of yours, make you scream for hours.

I felt my cheeks heat as I smiled to myself. My fingers tapped quietly against the keyboard as I typed out a response to yet another message from RomanticAlpha42. We had been messaging now for a solid two months. We'd barely missed a day. I hit send and relaxed back against my bed's headboard while I waited for a reply.

I flipped through the channels on the TV, and I'd just settled into an episode of *Outlander* when my phone rang.

"Hello," I whispered into the phone, trying to be

quiet, so I didn't disturb my father who was sure to be asleep by now.

"So has the love of your life, Mr. Spencer Brooks, or should I say RomanticAlpha42, confessed his love for you yet?" Carly giggled into the phone.

I rolled my eyes as I checked to see if I had any new messages but was quickly disappointed when I saw that nothing had come through. In fact, he hadn't even read what I'd sent back yet.

"It's just harmless fun. Plus, I don't even know if it's really him!" I replied as I watched the three little dots bounce on the screen letting me know he was typing something. Suddenly, a little check mark appeared on our chat, and I clicked to open the new message and read the words on my screen.

"I can't believe you're actually engaging with people on there." She laughed. "If you ask me, it's kind of creepy, talking to people you don't know."

Truth was, when my trial had expired, I'd let it lapse for two days, but then I was so curious to see if he would continue speaking with me that I ended up paying for a month, followed by another, and yet another because I was enjoying speaking with whoever it was I was speaking to so much. Deep down I'd prayed it was Spencer, but of course, I wouldn't ever know until I met the person—if I ever met the person.

"Not people," I corrected. "I'm only interacting with one person."

Carly let out a loud laugh. "Yeah, sorry about that. One person you believe to be Spencer. So, what does Mr. Romance have to say? Is he as smooth as you'd hoped?"

I had barely heard a word Carly had said as I read the message that sat on my screen. "Oh my God, you're not going to believe this."

"What? Trouble in paradise already?" Carly laughed.

"He's asked me to go on a date with him this coming weekend!" I answered.

"This weekend? As in Valentine's weekend?"

"Yes. Which, if this is Spencer, it would be to the Valentine's thing he is hosting, the one my father is going to be at." I kept reading his words repeatedly. "What do I do?"

"Ask him what he has in mind."

I quickly typed out what Carly told me to type and hit send. I only waited for a couple of seconds before a response came in. "He says not to worry, I would be perfectly safe, it would be a public event, nothing private."

"Interesting," Carly responded.

"What do I do now?"

"Well, since you are babysitting his daughter, you'll have to tell him no, or you could cancel on the little girl and explain to the real Spencer why it is you are canceling. However, I am sure it will be very uncomfortable when you give him your address, or perhaps when you meet up with him and you have to explain all over again. But you're a big girl. I am sure you will figure it out."

I swallowed hard as I tapped my fingers on the keyboard, debating what to respond with. "That isn't helpful, Carly."

"That's true. However, you haven't needed my help to get you this far, so I am sure you will figure it out." She giggled.

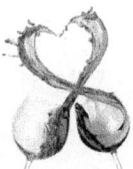

Spencer

This woman had me spinning, and I had no clue what she even looked like. I sat behind my desk awaiting a response from BabyGirl98. This was the exact reason why I loved the company I had created. It gave people the chance to get to know the real person without any outside judgment. I flipped between my email and back to my profile. I had sent off the date request almost forty minutes ago, and I knew that she had read it. It had never taken so long for a response from her to come through. Perhaps she wasn't interested.

I'd been out of the game so long I feared I might be losing my touch; although I had kept her online the past three nights engaged in some very heavy dirty talk, enough to even get a couple gratuitous photos sent my way, which while I waited for her response, I opened up.

I leaned back in my chair and stared at my screen, my cock throbbing as I flipped between the photos, when my phone rang. "Spencer Brooks."

"Hey, Spencer, what time are we leaving tonight?"

"Hey, Jon! Ainsley is coming by around seven, so I figure after I get Nikki settled with her, I guess we could leave around eight."

"Great!"

"Did you look at the package I dropped off for you?"

"I glanced at it but haven't had a chance to sit down and log into the computer or anything."

"Well, make sure you do. As I said, these aren't your run-of-the-mill women just looking to get laid. They are looking for meaningful relationships, and I have implemented a very rigorous screening process. Also to ease your mind, every account is 100% private. No one can see what you talk about."

"I'll check it out before we leave. Are you bringing a date tonight?"

"Hopefully a date with a very sexy twenty-year-old!"

"That sounds promising. I'll see you tonight then!"

"You got it."

I hung up the phone in time to see a message from BabyGirl89. I clicked open the message, excitement building in me, and leaned back in my chair.

BabyGirl89: RomanticAlpha42, I would love nothing more than to accompany you tonight.
However, I have a prior engagement that, unfortunately, I cannot get out of.
Until then, I will dream of you, BabyGirl89

RomanticAlpha42: To say I am disappointed is an understatement. Perhaps another time?

The three dots bounced around on the page, and before I knew it, a message appeared.

BabyGirl89: Absolutely. It's just bad timing.

I leaned back, disappointment filling me. After three months of talking, I was just a bit shocked at the answer I'd received, but it was really a last-minute thing and perhaps she was telling me the truth. Perhaps she really was busy.

I flipped from the chat screen over to my email and sent off a few end-of-the-day emails, then I began shutting things down and getting ready to head home. I was just about to log out of our chat screen when I noticed another message, titled 'Just for You'. I clicked it open and my jaw dropped.

I had to blink to make sure I wasn't seeing things, but when I opened my eyes, the picture was still there. She stood before the camera, almost naked, wearing only a sexy bra and panty set, but once again, there wasn't a picture of her face. My cock ached, and I reached down and placed my hand over it, squeezing it as I willed it to go down.

Spencer

I groaned out loud as shots of cum sprayed over my abs. This was the seventh time in twelve hours that I had jerked off thanks to BabyGirl89. We'd chatted late into the night, and the string of pictures she had sent to me once I'd gotten into bed had been permanently burned into my memory.

I reached for a tissue and had just finished cleaning up the sticky mess I had made when the doorbell rang. I grabbed another tissue, swiped it across my stomach, and reached for my T-shirt that was lying on the back of the desk chair, throwing it over my head. I tied the string on my gym shorts and pulled open my bedroom door, as I listened to Nikki scream for me.

"I got it, Nikki, don't worry," I called as I climbed down the three steps to the front door and pulled it open to see Ainsley standing there, a bag slung over her shoulder.

"Hey, Ains, come on in." She awkwardly smiled at me and stepped through the door. "Here, give me these," I said, reaching for her bags and setting them down on the upper step. "Oh and let me take your coat."

She turned, allowing me to slip her coat from her shoulders. I couldn't help but look down at her breasts, as they spilled out of the top of her low-cut shirt. I swallowed hard as she turned around to face me, and I took her coat and grabbed a hanger from the closet.

She wore a snug black T-shirt and tight jeans that perfectly molded to her tight, round ass. I couldn't help it, my eyes ran the length of her body, her long, shapely legs, perky tits that I'd love to bury my face in, and nipples hard enough that they called to me through her T-shirt. They'd been calling to me since last summer, every time I saw her sunbathing in her backyard.

I remembered the first time I had seen her sprawled out in her backyard. I had sat in the kitchen across from her father that same afternoon with a rock-hard cock as she came into the kitchen in that skimpy little bikini to get a drink. It was all I could do then to keep my eyes off her. That was the exact moment that I had begun this descent into imagining what it would be like to fuck Ainsley Matthews senseless. I imagined on more than one occasion what it would be like to have her legs wrapped around my neck, panting my name as I pounded relentlessly into her. It hadn't gotten any better either because after a year, I still imagined it. I imagined it was Ainsley every single time I spoke to BabyGirl89.

"Hey, Mr. ummm...Spencer. Where's Nikki?"

"In the kitchen coloring. Come on in. I'm just trying to finish getting ready. Nikki has been demanding today."

She toed her shoes off before she climbed the stairs and stopped beside me in the hallway. The smell of vanilla invaded my senses. "I see you brought a night bag."

"I did. I hope that's all right. I know I am just next door, but I figured it would be best in case you are late. I'll just sleep in the room attached to Nikki's, like I've done before. Oh, and I also brought some craft supplies, movies, and snacks for us ladies. I'll make sure that crafts stay in the kitchen, that way we won't get glue on anything." She looked up at me innocently.

"That's fine." I smiled, even though I instantly wanted to bend down and remove that look of innocence off her face. "I've got to finish getting ready."

"All right, we will be in the kitchen." Ainsley smiled, bent down, and picked up her bag and wandered toward the kitchen.

I couldn't help but watch as she walked away from me, taking that hot, sexy body with her. My eyes were glued to that perfect ass as it swayed back and forth. I felt my cock start to stir, and I knew in that instant that I had to tear my eyes from her. I began to make my way down to my bedroom when I heard Nikki's little voice filled with excitement.

"Oh, Spencer, that is just hilarious," Jenelle said as she ran her hand down my arm.

Jenelle had been after me all night. She had sat with me through dinner, approached me for a dance, and had hung on to my every word as I mingled with all the clients of *Finding Forever*.

"Please, excuse me for a few moments. I need to check on a private business matter," I lied and excused myself from the group. I was tired of being pawed. Women like Jenelle only took interest in me for one thing, and that was my wallet. I knew it, and they knew it as well.

I made a graceful exit, pretending I had seen someone off in the crowd, and quickly escaped the party. I snuck out of the conference room door and made my way up to my office where I closed the door and relished in the quiet. Sitting down at my desk, I removed my phone from my breast pocket, immediately pulling up my conversation with BabyGirl89, and sent out a message.

RomanticAlpha42: Wish you were here tonight. I would love nothing more than to have you on my arm.

BabyGirl89: I'd love nothing more also, but as I said, I have a previous engagement.

RomanticAlpha42: You're making me jealous; do you have a boyfriend?

BabyGirl89: If you must know, I am helping a friend out.

RomanticAlpha42: Is it a male friend

BabyGirl89: Yes

RomanticAlpha42: Why don't you send me something naughty

I smiled as I hit send. Minutes went by, and then an image populated my screen. My cock instantly hardened at the sight of her fingers inching their way into her black lace panties. I licked my lips and ran my hand over the thick, hard ridge that sat behind my suit pants. I felt like I was going to bust when another image populated my screen. This time I was faced with a panty-less, fully-shaven BabyGirl89. I swallowed hard and groaned as I squeezed my cock. As I studied the picture, I froze, noticing something familiar about the blanket that lay underneath her. I looked harder at the pattern in the blanket, instantly recognizing it as the blanket my great aunt had made me that lay on the bed in my spare guest room. I swallowed hard, only to see another message.

BabyGirl89: Are you there? Do you not like me?

I dropped my phone and turned on my computer, logging into the confidential client information area. I quickly searched for BabyGirl89, and within seconds, I was faced with every drop of her personal information. I scanned through it looking for anything that might be familiar. I didn't see anything that would lead me to believe it was, in fact, Ainsley, so I clicked over to the payment information and froze. Ainsley Matthews was the credit card holder. I swallowed hard, panic filling me for a second as I looked down at my phone at the pictures that had been sent. I picked up my phone and looked back up to the screen in front of me and thought for a second of what to reply.

BabyGirl89: Well?

I swallowed hard and closed my eyes. I picked up my

phone, looking back to the computer screen and staring at Ainsley's name. All the things I'd said to her, all the dirty, dirty things I'd said... What was worse was the fact that I had meant every single one of them. I took in a deep breath, then I slowly typed out my response.

RomanticAlpha42: I like you very much.

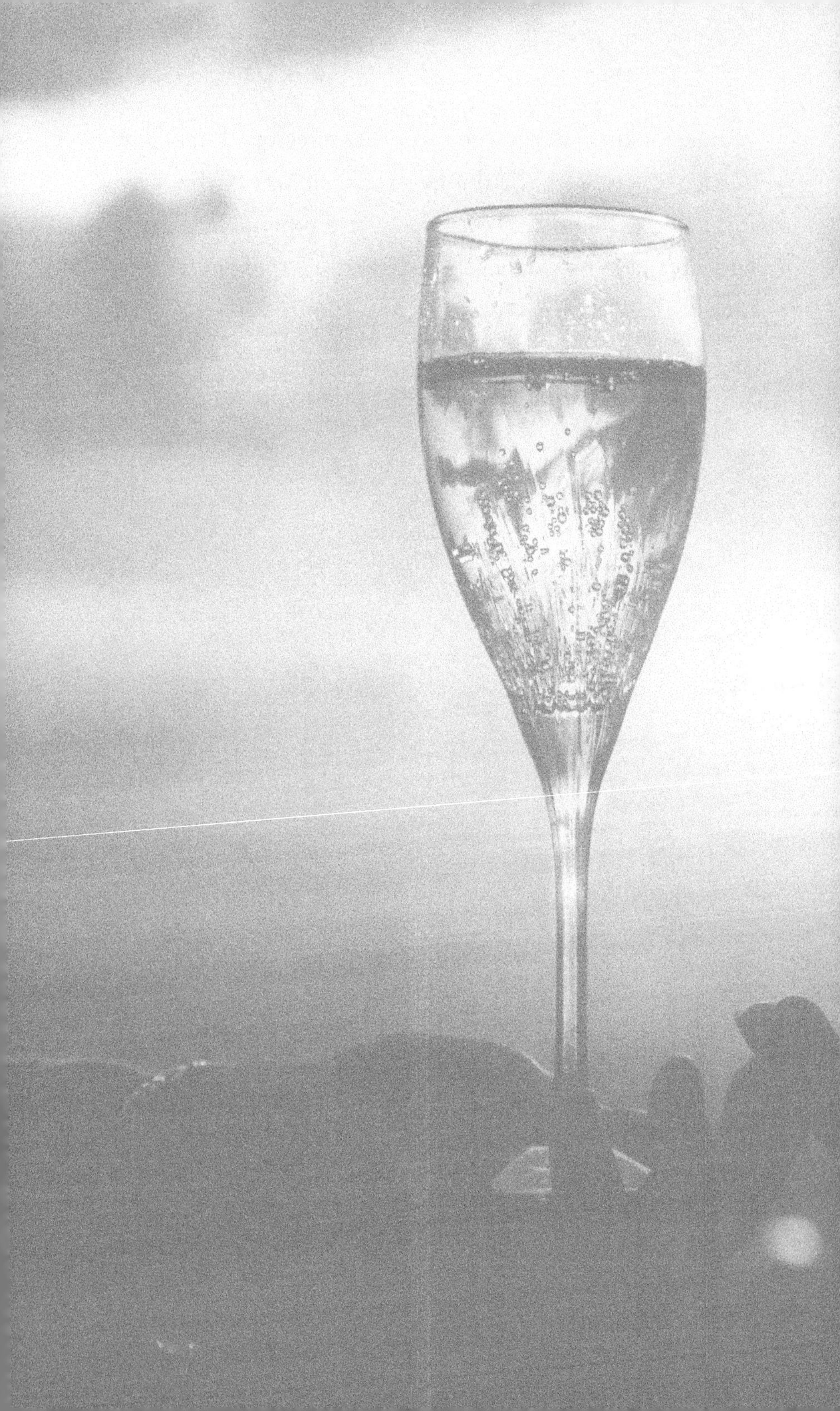

Spencer

After finding out it was indeed Ainsley I'd been talking to, I hadn't been able to look Jon in the face after I'd returned from my office. I'd seen him watching for me as I made my way through the crowd of people, but I ignored the fact and kept busy mingling with clients.

After everyone had left and the cleanup crew started, I made my way over to a bar down the street. I made my way in and sat down at the bar and ordered a scotch on the rocks. As soon as the golden liquid was placed down in front of me, I picked up the glass and took a sip. I had to figure out how to end this with her.

I'd said things to her, she'd sent things to me—things that neither of us should have shown or said to one another. Hell, she shouldn't even know some of those things, I thought to myself as I downed my drink and nodded to the bartender for another one. Then I pulled my phone from my pocket and went over our conversations. There would be no way I would have guessed it had been her, she seemed so mature for her age. There was no need to figure it all out right now, I thought to myself. I downed my drink, paid my bill, and made my way back to the office where I'd left my car.

I slowly turned into the driveway, put the car in park, shut the engine off, and glanced down at my watch. It was shortly after two. I hadn't planned on being this late, and I was surprised to see the soft glow of the living room light on through the front window.

Ainsley was still awake. I felt my heart start to accelerate as I opened the car door. I'd hoped she would be asleep. I walked up to the front door, put my key in the lock, and turned it, pushing the door open. I was quiet, doing my best not to disturb her in case she was asleep. *I prayed she was asleep.* I quietly took my shoes off and had just shrugged out of my suit jacket when I heard Ainsley's tired voice.

"Hello, Mr... I mean, Spencer. Is that you?"

I smiled to myself. Her sleepy voice was sexy as fuck. "Yeah, it's just me, Ainsley," I said, hanging my suit jacket on the banister and climbing the stairs to the living room.

I stopped in my tracks. Ainsley lay curled up on the couch, under a blanket, watching TV. As her eyes met mine, she quickly sat up, shoving the blankets off her, and my eyes fell to her bare legs.

"How did everything go tonight?" I questioned, swallowing hard. "Nikki be-have herself?"

"Nikki went to bed with no problem. I let her stay up a little later than normal. We were watching *Lady and the Tramp*. I hope that's okay."

"Sure." I smiled.

"How did tonight go for you?" she asked, gathering the blanket and folding it back up.

"It went well."

She smiled at me. "That's fantastic. I'm happy to hear that. Perhaps next year I will get to go to this event."

Yes, you will get to go next year, but you will go as my date, I thought to myself.

"Well, I should get going, let you get some sleep. It's late and Nikki told me you guys are off to the zoo in the morning. I'll just grab my things and be on my way."

Shit, I'd forgotten about the zoo. I pinched the bridge of my nose and then looked over to Ainsley who had her back to me as she threw the blanket onto the back of the couch.

"Ainsley, there's no rush." I turned and walked into the kitchen. "I was going to have a glass of wine. Would you care for one?" Every single part of me knew that I was crossing a line by asking her to join me. Hell, I had crossed a line by even speaking with her for the past couple of months. Granted, I hadn't known it was her.

I pulled the bottle from the fridge and turned to see her leaning against the doorway. What was I doing? I had decided to end this with her, not invite her to have wine with me. I had to end it; this was ridiculous. After all, she was going to be working for me soon, and I had a strict no fraternization policy in my company.

I pulled at my tie, loosening it from my neck, and unbuttoned the top three buttons of my shirt as I watched her eyes wash over me, her cheeks flushed while she bit her bottom lip. *God I'd love to make her bite that bottom lip, better yet, I'd love to bite it.*

"Um...okay...I guess one glass won't hurt. Can I help you with anything?" I noticed she swallowed hard as she looked around the room.

"I'm fine. Why don't you go sit down? I will bring the wine in." I winked at her and watched as she left to go back into the living room. As soon as she left the room, I pulled my phone from my pocket and sent a message to BabyGirl89. I needed to know if, in fact, it was her, and there was no other way I would ever find out. I couldn't ask her. After all, I was sure there were other Ainsley Matthews in the world. I hit send and placed two glasses on the counter. I reached into the fridge and pulled the bottle of wine out, and that was when I heard her phone give off a notification.

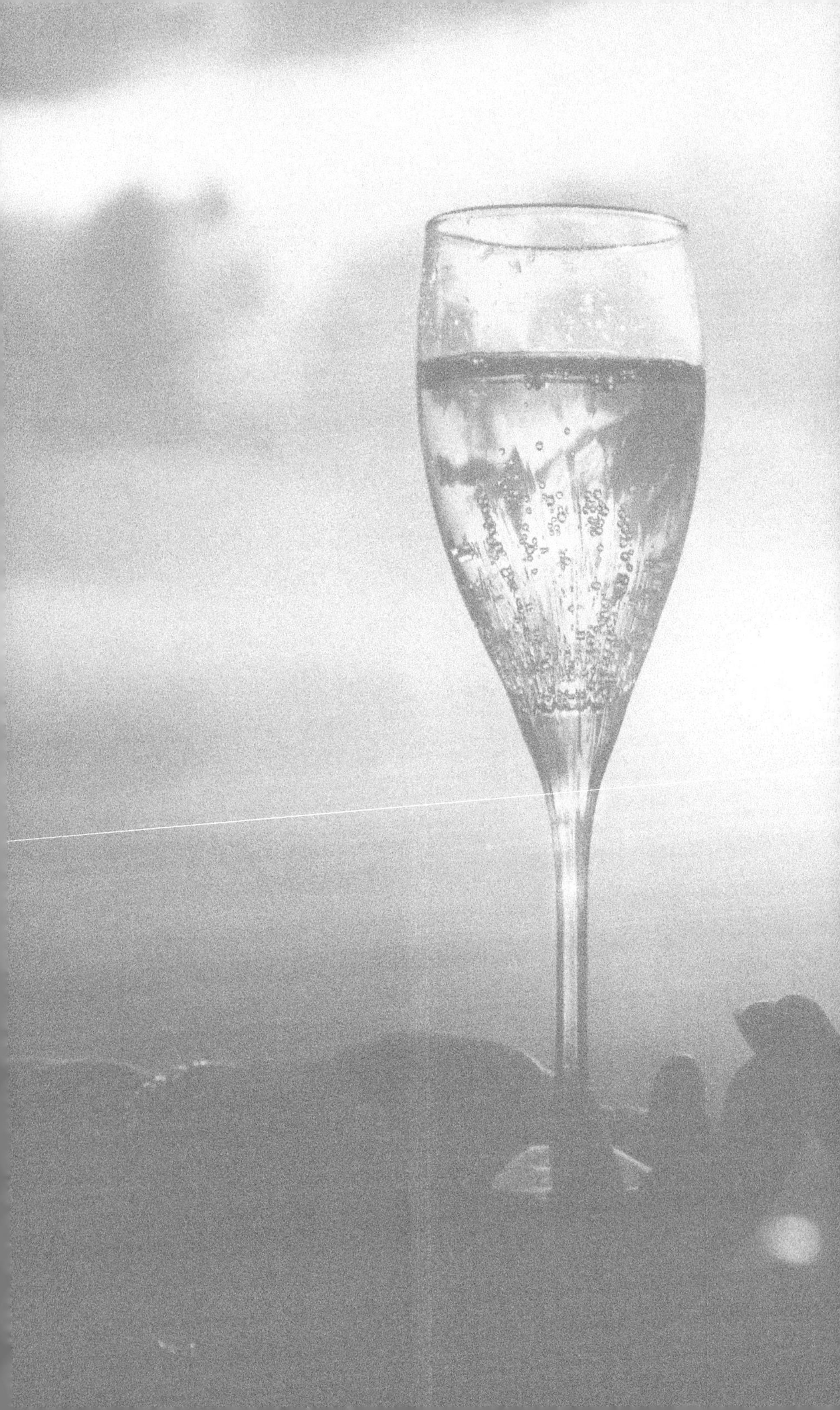

Ainsley

I wandered into the living room and took a seat in the same spot I'd been in when Spencer had come in. I curled my feet underneath me and relaxed into the plush cushions. I'd just gotten comfortable when my phone went off. I grabbed it from the table and stared at the screen, biting my bottom lip.

RomanticAlpha42: You busy?

"Fuck," I muttered. If RomanticAlpha42 truly was Spencer, I wondered if there was a way that he could find out that BabyGirl89 was me. I tapped the edge of my phone and bit my bottom lip while I listened to Spencer continue to bang around in the kitchen.

"Did you want anything to eat? Cheese and crackers perhaps?" he called out.

"Um...sure," I answered while I quickly typed my response. I'd hoped that would stall him until I could figure out if it truly was Spencer.

BabyGirl89: Just heading to bed.

As I hit send, I listened hard and heard Spencer's ringtone go off. My stomach flipped with nerves, and suddenly the room got very warm. Almost instantly, my phone went off again.

RomanticAlpha42: Are you going to bed alone?

BabyGirl89: I wish I didn't have to say yes, but sadly yes.

I bit my bottom lip, and when I heard his phone go off again, I knew I had to get out of here. RomanticAlpha42 was Spencer. Carly was right, I'd played with fire, and I was about to get burned. Then, as if my brain hadn't registered what I had done, I recalled each picture I had sent him. Pictures of me that...well, pictures of me that should never have been sent, should never have been seen, and embarrassment flooded me. Shit, I should have listened to Carly.

I looked around the room, remembering that my bags were already in the spare room down the hall. "Fuck," I whispered under my breath, debating if I had time to make it to the spare room to get my stuff before I left. As panic built, I flew to the front door, my phone going off once again in my pocket. I fought to get one shoe on and pulled my phone from my pocket, looking down to see a message from RomanticAlpha42 on my screen.

RomanticAlpha42: That's too bad BabyGirl. I'd gladly join you if I were there.

I slipped my phone back into my pocket and picked up my shoe, my hands shaking so bad that I immediately dropped it back to the floor. I bent to pick it up, and that was when I heard Spencer clear his throat.

I froze and slowly turned to see him leaning against the wall looking sexier than I'd ever seen him. He had completely removed his tie. His shirt was undone and hung open enough that I could see his chest. His shirtsleeves were rolled up, exposing his muscular forearms. I felt that familiar ache beginning between my legs. An ache that I had felt so many other times seeing him like this. He stood there holding a glass of wine in one hand and his phone in the other, a sexy smirk on his face.

I turned back around and grabbed my shoe from the floor and went to put it on when I heard Spencer clear his throat again.

"Ainsley?"

I stopped moving and swallowed hard. "Yes?"

"Where are you going?"

I fought back my embarrassment and pulled the front door open. I still didn't have my other shoe on; I still held it in my hand as the cold night air hit my face, instantly cooling me. I was about to step out onto the stoop when I felt his strong hand grip my arm. Fire lit inside of me, and instantly, I could feel the heat coming off him as he stepped forward, closing the space between us. When I felt the puff of his breath on the back of my neck, chills ran through my body. I closed my eyes as he leaned into me and whispered in my ear, "It's okay, you don't need to run from me, BabyGirl."

I stood frozen. I couldn't speak, I couldn't move, every nerve in body was on overdrive as he slid his arm around my waist, his large hand resting on my abdomen as he pulled me back against him. I hadn't expected my body to respond to him this way.

He shut the front door, locking it. "You don't need to run from me," he whispered again, and that was when I felt his hard, rigid cock press into me from behind as his lips lightly danced over the side of my neck.

My hands shook as they ran over his forearms. I breathed in his scent, and I closed my eyes as his lips continued to caress over my skin, relishing in the fact that Spencer Brooks was kissing me.

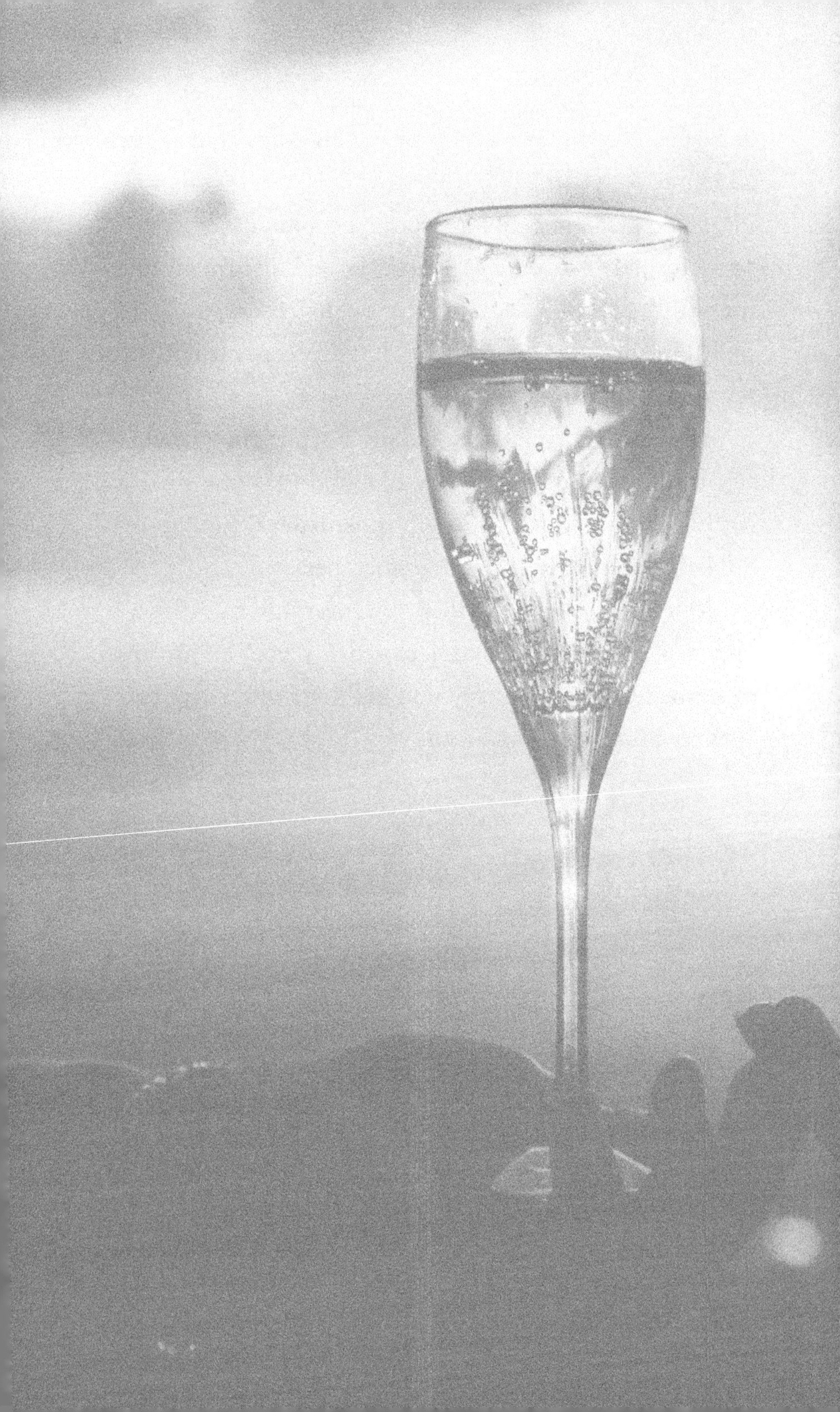

Spencer

I was intoxicated by her vanilla scent as my lips skimmed along her soft, sweet neck. I could feel her body tremor slightly the longer my lips grazed her neck. I placed my hand on the flat of her belly, and a soft moan escaped her lips. I turned her into me and pulled her against my chest, my hands gripping her hips. Once she was against me, I noticed she had finally stopped shaking.

I pushed her back up against the front door and pressed my body against hers. I ran my hand over her cheek and looked down into those sweet brown eyes and ran my thumb over her full, pouty, pink lips, her tongue jutting out to wet them. I bent slowly, taking her mouth with mine.

"I shouldn't have...I'm sorry," she murmured as my lips left hers.

"Shhhh, don't be sorry. I'm not. Do you not see the way I look at you, because I've seen the way you look at me, always full of want," I whispered, my hands gripping her ass and pulling her against me so she could feel just how not sorry I was. I met her lips and kissed her deeply, my tongue parting her lips.

In one swift motion, I picked her up, her legs quickly wrapping around my waist, and I pushed her against the wall, pinning her there, her arms around my neck, her fingers running through my hair.

"You know what I want to see," I whispered as I licked and sucked her earlobe and listened to that sexy little moan of hers.

"What?" she asked breathlessly as I continued kissing my way down her neck.

I looked at her, wanting to see her reaction. "That sweet pussy, the one you've been teasing me with for months."

Her cheeks reddened at my answer. "I haven't," she answered breathlessly between kisses.

She wrapped her fingers in my hair, gripping as she kissed me. When the next soft moan escaped her lips, I carried her upstairs and headed down the hall toward my bedroom.

I placed her gently down on the edge of my bed, and she looked up at me with innocent eyes. I unbuttoned my shirt, her eyes washing over me, the flush on her cheeks beautiful as she bit her bottom lip. She sat there staring back at me, unsure of what she should do.

I grabbed the hem of her shirt and pulled it up and over her head, tossing it over in the corner. I was surprised when I felt her grab my belt and nervously fumble with the buckle. Once undone, she pulled at the button on my dress pants, which I finished undoing myself, my cock aching for her hands, her mouth, whatever she wanted to use.

There was something so innocent about the way she looked at me, at my erection. I placed my hand under her chin, bringing her eyes to mine. At first, I wasn't sure she was even going to touch me, and then I nearly came right on the spot as she brought her hand to my boxers and gripped my hardened shaft through the material.

I closed my eyes and steadied my breathing. There was no way I could embarrass myself in front of her by coming early. I pushed her back, ripping the cups of her bra down and exposing her perfect tits. Her nipples were already hard, calling to me. I knelt down onto the bed and sucked one into my mouth, gently teasing her with little nibbles. Her moan echoed loudly through the room.

"Ainsley, shhhh, you'll wake Nikki," I whispered.

I took the other in my mouth, doing the same thing and getting the same response. God I loved the way she sounded. I kissed my way down the flat of her stomach and gripped the waistband of her shorts, inching them off along with her panties, kissing every bare inch of her body as I went.

Finally, once those were gone, I spread her legs and kneeled on the floor. I spread them as far as they would go. She was already glistening, and I had barely touched her. I kept my hands firmly placed on the insides of her thighs so she couldn't close her legs and ran my tongue right through her center. Her hands gripped my duvet tightly as she struggled not to make a sound. I repeated what I had just done, this time my tongue flicking against her swollen clit. This time she couldn't contain it, and her cries went straight to my cock.

I reached into the drawer of my nightstand and pulled a condom out. "Fuck, I want to bury myself inside of you," I murmured as I ran my tongue through her again. I sat back, ripping the package open and rolling it down my cock.

I crawled up between her legs, kneeling on the bed. I slipped one finger then two deep inside of her, my thumb gently circling her clit. She was tight, and the more I circled her clit, the tighter she gripped my fingers as she began to whimper. Instantly, I kissed her to hush those cries that continued to send a shiver through my body.

I pulled my fingers from her and lined myself up at her entrance and pumped my hard, aching cock a couple of times, then I gripped her hips to hold her still and met her lips one more time.

I eased the head of my cock into her and heard her whimper as she dug her fingernails into my back. She was tighter than I imagined, and I had to take a breath before I continued.

"You okay, BabyGirl?" I whispered, waiting for her to adjust to me before I fully buried myself into her. It was all I could do to hold back and not come instantly as I pushed myself into her and she bit into my shoulder to keep from moaning too loud. As soon as I knew she had adjusted to me, I began pumping into her as I held her tightly.

I placed her legs on my shoulders and buried myself as deep as I could go, and she let out a loud moan. I pumped hard and deep, gripping her hips as she closed her eyes and bit her lip, trying hard to be quiet. I could feel her tightening around me. The tighter she got, the harder it was for me to hold back, and soon I could feel my balls tightening. She came first, hard and loud, and I followed, emptying myself into the condom.

I stayed deep inside of her until the pulsing stopped, and then I slipped from inside of her. As I walked across the room to the bathroom, I already missed her body. I got rid of the condom and then took a minute to heat a cloth. I carried it into the bedroom to find her laying spent on the bed.

I crawled in beside her, placing the warm cloth between her legs, gently cleaning her. Then I dropped the cloth beside the bed, pulled the covers back, and slipped my arm under her neck, pulling her close to me.

Ainsley lay in my arms, her head resting on my chest, her warm body against mine. I kissed her gently and ran my hand over her hip, relishing in the softness of her skin. I could already feel my cock starting to stir at the thought of how she fit so perfectly against me. I never wanted the night to end, and I glanced to the clock to see how much time we had left together.

She started to stir in my arms, and I placed a gentle kiss on her forehead and closed my eyes. We had plenty of time before morning. I'd almost drifted off to sleep when I heard a shrill scream from the other room.

"DAAAAAAADDDDDDYYYYY."

My heart thudded hard in my chest, as panic filled me at the thought of Nikki coming into this room to find us together.

"DDDDDAAAAAAADDDDDDDYYYYYY," she cried out again.

I pulled my arm out from under Ainsley's body and sat up, picking up my boxers from the floor and pulling them on. "Wha...What's going on? Where are you going?"

Ainsley murmured, lifting her head from the pillow and looking at me with sleepy eyes.

"Shhhh....go to sleep. It's just Nikki. I've got to go check on her. I'll be right back."

I left Ainsley and went down the hall and into Nikki's room to find her crying in her bed. I picked her up and held her close to me, sitting down with her until she fell back asleep, then I made my way back to my bedroom.

I opened the door quietly, expecting to find Ainsley still asleep, but instead, I found her sitting on the edge of the bed, fully dressed. The second I closed the door, she stood up and turned away from me.

"Ainsley, is everything okay?" I swallowed hard as I walked up behind her and placed my hands on her arms. As soon as I touched her, she was flooded with emotion.

"What is it, what's wrong?" I questioned.

"This was not a wise choice." Her voice was thick with emotion.

"DAAAAADDDDDYYYY," Nikki cried out again from the other room.

"Fuck," I muttered under my breath. "Give me a minute."

"No, Spencer, I have to go," she cried, her eyes brimming with tears.

"Please. Don't go anywhere. Just give me a minute, please," I begged.

It took me ten minutes to get Nikki back to sleep

before I could finally return to my bedroom. I was afraid she would have left, gone home to her bedroom where she would be out of my reach. However, when I opened the bedroom door, I was pleasantly surprised to see her sitting on opposite side of the bed, her back to me.

"Now, onto you," I said as I clicked the door shut and walked around the bed, kneeling between her legs. "What's going on in that pretty head of yours?" I asked, brushing a loose strand of hair from her face.

She avoided eye contact with me at first, looking everywhere but at me. Then she took in a deep breath and met my eyes. "It's just...we shouldn't have," she said, glancing back to the bed. "What if my father finds out?"

I looked at her and chuckled, then quit. I didn't want her to think I was making fun of her worries, because that wasn't what I was doing. She had every right to be worried, but she also needed to know that I wasn't about to go talking to her father about this. "This...what went on here tonight, is our little secret. If you want it to stop, it stops, no questions asked," I whispered, leaning in to kiss her. "If you want it to continue, then it continues. You say that word, BabyGirl. You're in control here, no one else, just you."

I could still see a lot of uncertainty in her eyes. "What is it?"

"What about you? Don't you have a say?"

I shook my head. I had no right to have a say. "You are in control. You say what you want," I repeated.

She studied my face, my eyes, my lips, and slowly she leaned in and kissed me, slowly at first, and then with a little more passion.

"I take it that means you want more?."

She nodded her head and smiled at me, wrapping her arms around my neck.

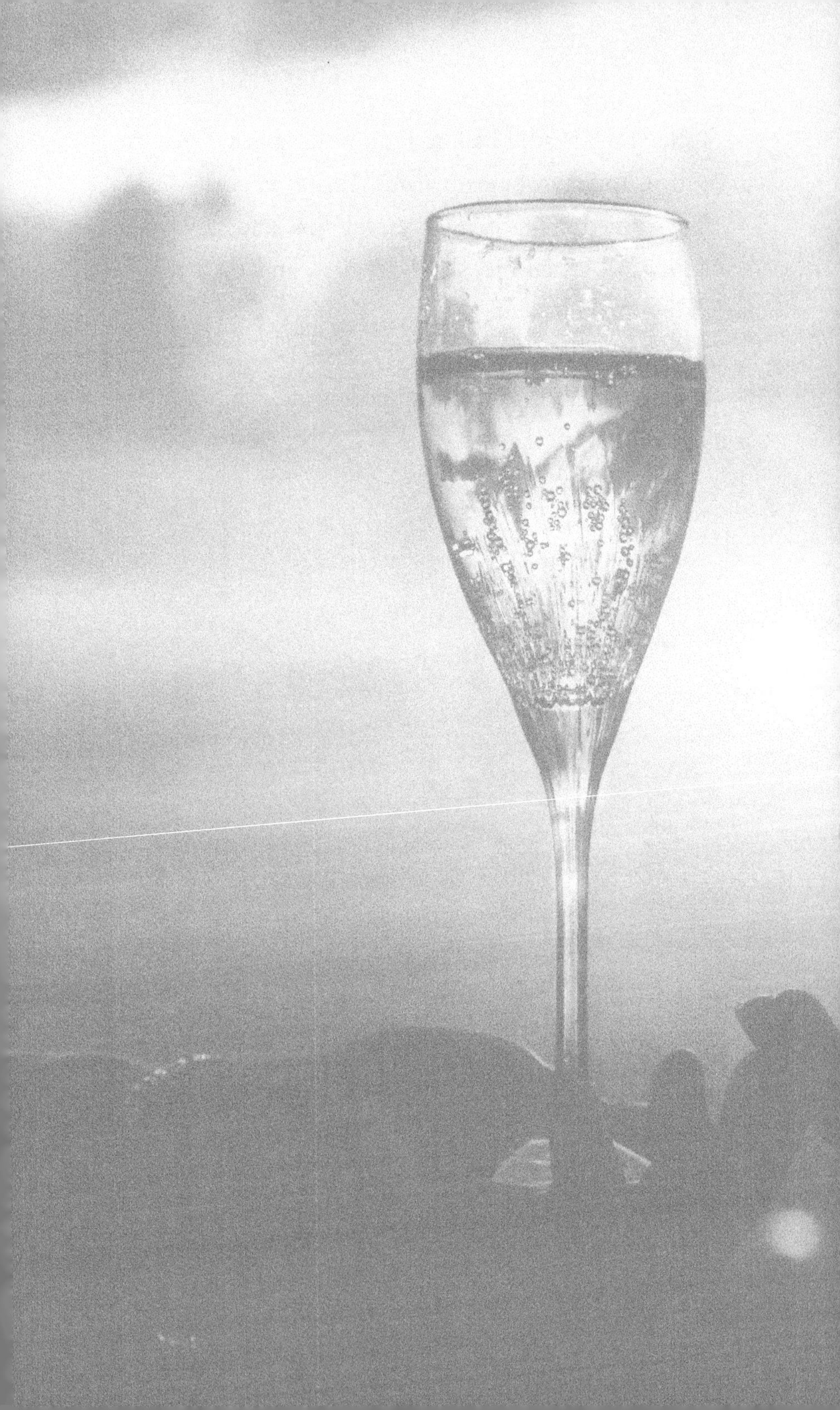

Ainsley

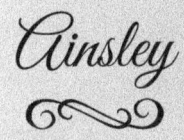

I lay curled up under my blankets watching TV. It was after ten, and I was exhausted from the night I'd spent with Spencer. I'd tried all day, but I hadn't been able to shut my head off. My mind continuously floated to what had happened between us. My father had asked me numerous times how the night had gone, and I had just shrugged and given him my usual answer: that Nikki had behaved, and Spencer had gotten home late, so I'd spent the night. Only, this was the first time I had noticed my father looked at me strangely.

I closed my eyes. I could still feel his hands on my body. I could feel myself getting aroused as I remembered how his lips felt against my neck.

"Ainsley, I'm heading to bed," my father said, poking his head into my room.

Alarm filled me for a moment as I opened my eyes, my father standing there watching me. I swallowed hard. "Okay, have a good night's sleep."

"You too, baby girl."

My body flooded with heat at the sound of my username on *Finding Forever*. My eyes opened wide, but my father was already gone, then something switched inside of me as I remembered my father had called me that since I'd been a little girl, and I giggled to myself at my moment of panic. *Why had I chosen that name for my username?* I lay back against my pile of pillows and reached for my remote control when my phone vibrated.

I smiled to myself as I looked at the screen.

RomanticAlpha42: I can't stop thinking of you.

I quickly hit reply and bit my bottom lip as I typed.

BabyGirl89: Same here, all I can think about is your hands, your lips, your tongue.

RomanticAlpha42: Is that all?

BabyGirl89: What?

RomanticAlpha42: Is that all you miss?

I sat there staring at his message, a smile on my face.

BabyGirl89: No

RomanticAlpha42: Tell me what else you miss?

I bit my bottom lip again as my body heated at the memory of him sliding his large, thick cock into me. I began typing and then quickly deleted what I'd typed. Then I tapped the side of my phone, retyping the words. I stared down at the message, then I hit send before I had time to think about it.

BabyGirl89: I miss your cock.

I sat biting on my thumb as I waited for his response, yet nothing came. Had I crossed a line by saying that, I wondered to myself. I had no idea how many times he had said those dirty things to me, but now my imagination was running wild, until I saw the three little dots begin to jump around as he typed.

RomaticAlpha42: You have no idea how much I miss that pussy of yours.

RomaticAlpha42: Want to have a little fun?

RomaticAlpha42: Hit the little call button down at the bottom of the chat area.

BabyGirl89: What does that do?

RomaticAlpha42: Press it and find out.

I pressed the call button and was shocked to see Spencer appear on my phone. He lay on his bed, shirtless, looking sexy as hell with his hand behind his head as he stared into the camera.

"I can't chat. I'll wake my dad," I whispered.

"Do you have headphones?"

I bit my bottom lip as I nodded.

"Get them."

I reached over to my nightstand and grabbed my headphones, quickly plugging them into the bottom of my phone. Then I slipped one of the ear pieces into my ear. That way I could listen for my dad.

"Can you hear me. Just nod if you can."

I nodded.

"Okay. I want you to do as I tell you, okay."

Once again, I nodded.

"I want you to get comfortable. What are you wearing?"

I kicked the covers off and ran the camera the length of my body so he could see my T-shirt and pajama pants.

"Remove your T-shirt and your pants, but if you have panties on, leave them on."

I swallowed hard and put the phone down beside me as I removed my shirt and quickly slid out of my pants. Throwing them on the floor, I quickly picked my phone back up, careful to keep any part of my body from the camera.

"I want you to imagine me being there with you. Take your free hand and slide your fingers over your right nipple."

I did as he asked, my nipples instantly getting hard at my touch. I opened my eyes and looked at the screen, at Spencer as he lay there.

"Now, slide your hand into your panties," his deep voice commanded.

At first, I hesitated, but then I slid my hand down the flat of my stomach to the waistband of my panties. I angled the camera lower so that Spencer could see as I slid my fingers inside of them.

"Now I want you to rub yourself for me, like I rubbed you. Just glide your fingers over yourself, teasing."

His voice was breathless as I did as he instructed. I angled my phone back up so I could see Spencer through what I was sure was lust-filled eyes.

"God, Ainsley, you're so hot," he murmured before flashing his camera down to his large, thick cock he held in his hand. He lay there stroking himself, which only turned me on more.

"Apply more pressure, Ainsley. Just enough, no more."

I did as he instructed. I could feel pressure beginning to build as I continued, first in slow, small, light circles, then harder and faster.

I watched as Spencer's muscles tightened in his chest and neck, as he continuously stroked himself. It would only be a matter of second before I would explode.

"Keep going, Ainsley. I want to hear you come."

I bit my bottom lip to keep myself from screaming as my orgasm ripped through me at the same time Spencer's ripped through him. I dropped my phone on my bed as I lay there breathing hard.

As soon as I had come down, I pulled my blankets over top of me and grabbed my phone, expecting to see Spencer's face, but the video call had gone dark. I was about to press it again when suddenly those three little familiar dots began to jump around.

RomaticAlpha42: That was hot as fuck. I wish I could have been there.

BabyGirl89: How about tomorrow night I leave my window open?

RomaticAlpha42: Don't tempt me. That might get me arrested ;) Good night BabyGirl.

Just like that, Spencer was gone, logged out for the night, leaving me all alone with my thoughts. I lay back on my bed, placed my phone on my nightstand, and took in a deep breath, trying to calm my beating heart. I had no idea what I had gotten myself into, but whatever it was, I was going to enjoy the ride.

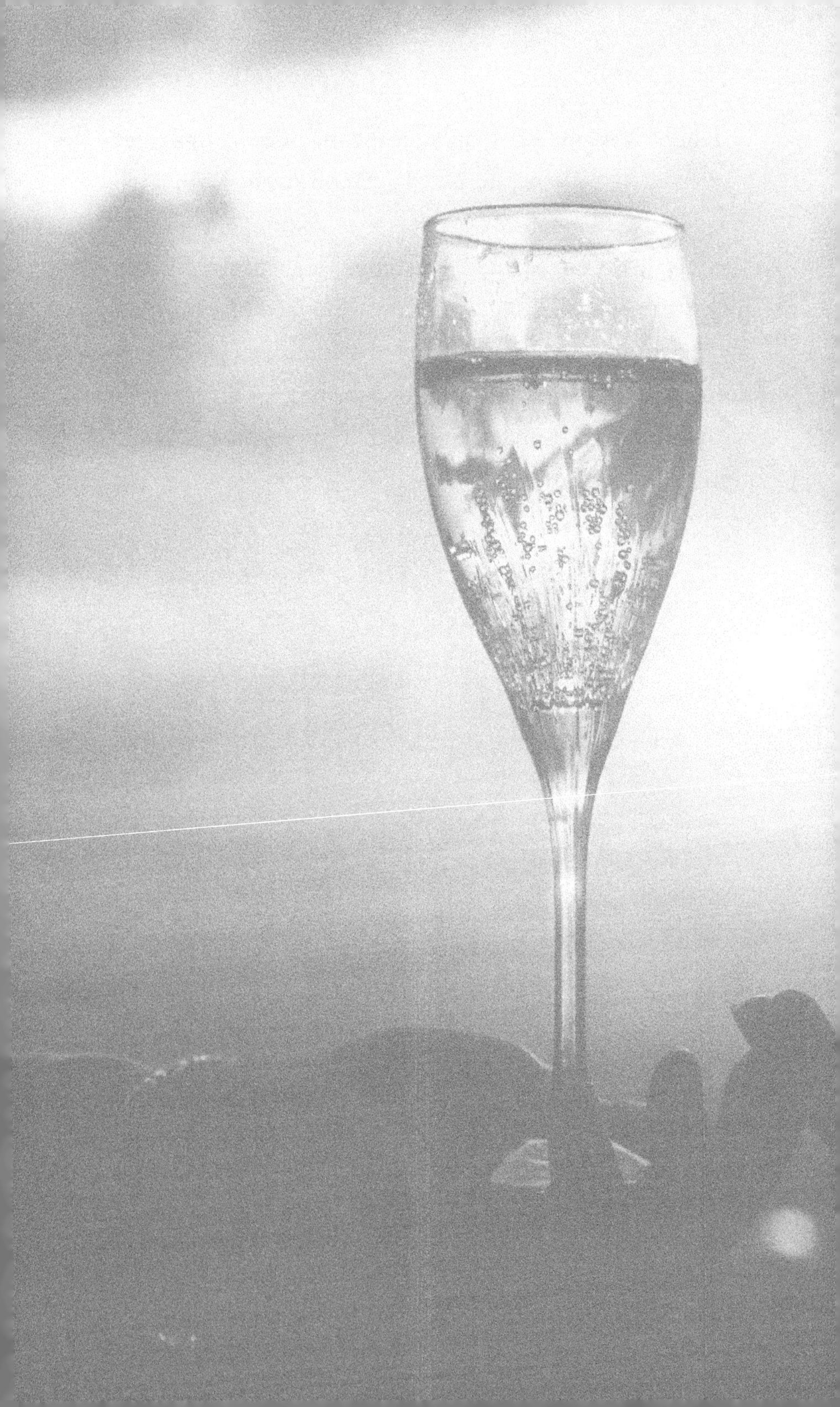

Ainsley: One Week Later

It was midafternoon the following Sunday, I was on the phone with Carly, and I watched from my bedroom window as Spencer came walking up the walkway to our front door, carrying a box of beer and what appeared to be a bottle of wine. I'd barely heard from him the entire week, except for Thursday afternoon for five minutes when he'd messaged me to see if I could run next door and see if he had locked his front door.

I listened with half an ear as Carly went on and on about some guy she was seeing. When the doorbell rang, I jumped and listened hard at my bedroom door for my father to answer.

"Carly, I've got to go."

"No fair, I was just getting ready to ask you all about

RomanticAlpha42. You haven't spoken about him all week."

"There is nothing to tell, to be honest. I guess the fizzle wore out," I lied as I heard the doorbell ring and heard both my father's voice and Spencer's.

"That's too bad. I was seriously hoping for some Spencer stories."

"I'm sure you were, but considering it wasn't Spencer, I don't have any stories to tell," I lied. "I'll call you later, okay."

"Ainsley, are you okay?" Carly questioned.

"Yeah why?"

"Just making sure. I know how badly you wanted it to be Spencer."

I swallowed hard. I wanted to tell her all about it. I hated lying to my best friend, but it was something that had to be done for now. There was no way I could risk even her finding out what had happened between us.

"I'll talk to you later, okay." I hung up the phone and made my way downstairs. "Smells good, Dad," I said, stepping into the kitchen and coming face-to-face with Spencer. He smiled softly at me.

"Thanks. Roast beef tonight. I invited Spencer to join us for dinner. I hope you don't mind."

"Why would I mind," I questioned, looking over at him, my cheeks heating as his eyes ran over me.

"I just figured you might. After all, Sunday night dinner has always been our night together," Dad replied.

"It's fine," I replied and walked over to the cupboard as Dad and Spencer continued their conversation they'd been having before I'd arrived. I was about to reach for a water glass when I heard Spencer clear his throat.

"I brought a bottle of wine for you, Ainsley. It's in the fridge."

"Thank you," I said, looking over my shoulder in Spencer's direction. He got up and grabbed the bottle of wine from the fridge. I dug around in the drawer for our wine opener and switched out my water glass for one of my new stemless wine glasses.

"Shit, I forgot to get something from the car. I'll be right back" my dad said, placing the roast back in the oven and grabbing his car keys from the hook by the door.

Seconds after my father had left the house, I felt Spencer's hands on my arms and his lips at the back of my neck. I closed my eyes as he pressed his lips to my neck, and then I turned to meet them, and that was when the front door crashed.

He pulled away from me, letting out a low, frustrated growl, and tore the wine bottle from my hand and began shoving the corkscrew into the cork, opening the wine for me.

"Forgot dessert," Dad said, ignoring us both and opening the fridge to put the dessert inside.

"How's things going with that chick?" Spencer asked my father as he sat back down, not taking his eyes from me, but doing his best to keep my father distracted.

"Great, we have another date next week. You were right, Spencer. I don't know why it took me so long to sign up."

"What about you, Spence, how are things? You find anyone yet?" Dad asked while tending to the roast in the oven, once again ignoring the pair of us.

Spencer cleared his throat and looked over to where I stood, watching me as he brought his beer bottle to his lips. "Um, I think I have."

I glanced to Spencer, wondering what the hell he was doing.

"And?" my father asked.

"She is amazing, but I don't want to jinx it."

I felt the flush on my cheeks as he looked over at me, but I had to look away.

"That is great, Spencer, really. You'll have to show me a picture of her. Or better yet, perhaps we could set up a double date."

I picked up my cell phone and quickly typed out a message, giving him shit, and hit send, Spencer's phone going off a second later. "I don't have one on me right now. Perhaps later," he lied as he typed a reply on his phone.

I pulled my phone from my pocket and noticed a

message from RomanticAlpha42 on my screen. I clicked it open and sucked in a full breath.

RomanticAlpha42: Perhaps you won't be so mad at me when I lick that sweet pussy later.

"Ainsley, everything okay?" Dad asked, taking a drink of his beer.

"What...Yep! Just Carly," I lied, taking a drink of my wine, almost chocking as it hit the back of my throat. I quickly typed out another message. Spencer's phone went off almost immediately. I had to get out of the kitchen before Dad caught on. "I'll be in my room," I murmured, taking my wine with me.

"Ainsley, we have company," my father gritted, annoyed with my behavior.

"Just let me deal with this. I'll be right down," I said, waving my hand at my father.

I walked into the living room and stood up against the wall in the hallway while I listened to my father as he rambled on to Spencer about Kate, the woman he had been seeing. I poked my head around the corner and watched Spencer read the message I had sent. As soon as he replied, my phone went off again, and I took off down the hall, pulling my phone out of my pocket as soon as I got into my room.

RomanticAlpha42: My place tonight, after your father has gone to bed. I'll make sure he is good and drunk by the time I leave, so you've got nothing to worry about!

I smiled to myself and typed out a response, agreeing to meet him. Then I quickly called Carly back then threw my phone down on my bed, grabbed my wine, and returned to join Dad and Spencer.

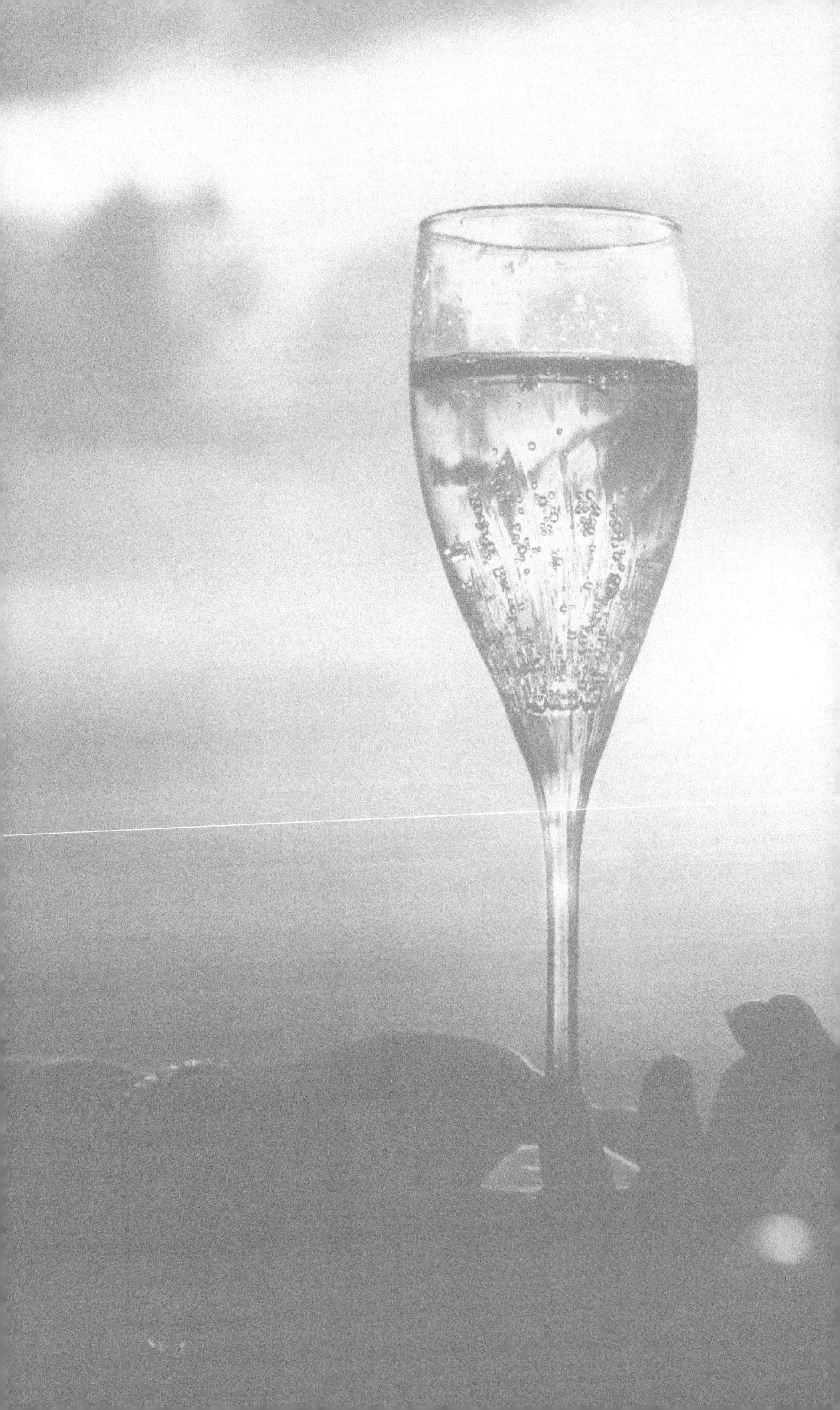

Spencer – Three Month's Later

To say I enjoyed working beside Ainsley more than my sixty-year-old assistant was an understatement. I leaned back in my chair and watched Ainsley through my partially opened office door, just like I'd done every night at this time. Today though was different. She looked absolutely amazing today. The dark sweater she wore clung to every curve, and paired with her black skirt, it took very little imagination on my part to picture her naked. She really needed to stop wearing office attire that made it hard for me to concentrate.

Suddenly, she looked up in my direction, and I quickly turned my attention back to the email I'd received early this morning. I was looking at expanding *Finding Forever* and was looking at opening a new office in Denver. I looked to the email I'd received earlier this morning from the real estate agent I'd contacted about office space; she could meet with me next week.

I tapped my fingers on the desk, fighting within myself. I figured this would be the perfect opportunity to get Ainsley alone for an entire weekend. I just needed to come up with a reason as to why I would need my assistant with me for such a thing. It wasn't because of a business decision. Hell, I ran the company. I could place funds wherever I needed. It was more because of Jon. He didn't understand the corporate world, and also didn't understand the need for me to keep Ainsley working so late most nights of the week. He had made more comments to me about her hours in the recent days.

I reached for the hot cup of coffee she had brought me ten minutes ago and took a sip, leaning back against my chair as I stared at her once again. The only thing on my mind was how I was going to convince her to come away with me.

I leaned forward and hit the extension for her desk. "Ainsley, could you come here for a moment please," I said, letting go of the intercom button on the phone.

Seconds later, she stood at my door. "Yes, Spencer?"

"Come in, close the door, please."

She shut the door behind her and approached my desk. "What did you need?" she questioned, giving me that innocent smile.

I couldn't take my eyes off her, my mind instantly

traveling back to two nights ago when I'd taken her on my desk. That night had started all because of that exact same smile. I smiled, picked up my mug, and took another sip.

"I heard back from that realtor in Denver. The one I had you contact about that office space."

"That is exciting. And..."

"Yes, and they have a few available spaces for me to check out, so I'll need a hotel booked. We have a corporate account at the Marriott. You should be able to find all the information in the binder Mary left for you, so, if possible, could you please book one for me for next Friday?"

She stepped forward, her eyes meeting mine as she leaned across my desk, the V-neck of her sweater falling open just enough for me to catch a glimpse of her full breasts. She grabbed the pad of sticky notes that sat in front of me then grabbed a pencil, met my eyes with a teasing glance, and smiled before scribbling a note down. "Anything else."

I clenched my jaw at the playfulness in her eyes.

"I'd like a king bed, jacuzzi room, and dinner reservations for Saturday night at a steak house near the hotel."

I watched as she made more notes on the small square note before glancing up at me. "How many people will be attending the dinner so I can make the appropriate reservation?"

"Make it for two people." Her eyes lifted from the

paper, meeting mine, and I was sure I saw a hint of jealousy in them, but she proceeded to give me a soft smile.

"For two..." her voice hitched as she stared at the note. "Okay, I'll get that booked right away," she said, turning and heading to the door. She'd just pulled the door open then abruptly turned around.

"Oh, before I forget, you have a meeting with the IT department in thirty minutes. Shall I set up the boardroom and order in lunch?"

I quickly clicked over to my calendar and saw that my entire afternoon had been booked with this meeting, the only one I'd forgotten about. "Please, assorted wraps from Mario's is fine."

"Very well, I'll have them dropped in at twelve thirty."

"Thank you. Oh, and, Ainsley, this meeting is probably going to go into the early evening. Are you able to stay a little later tonight so I can go over a few things with you?"

Ainsley nodded, then smiled before pulling my door shut.

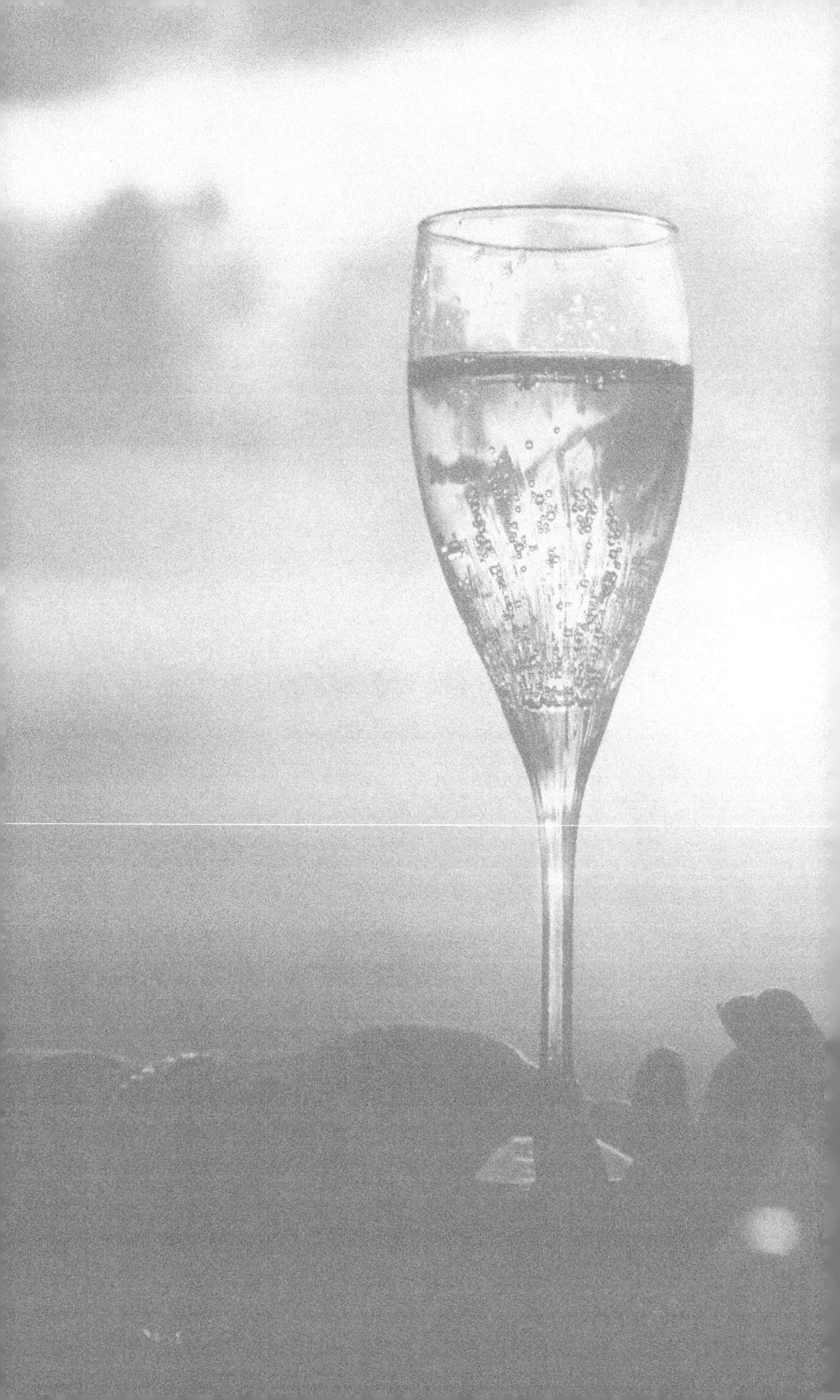

Ainsley

It was a little after eight. The other two people who worked on this floor had already left for the night. I glanced down the hall at the boardroom door. It was still tightly shut. No one had come out of that room since I'd gone in at five with a fresh thermos of coffee, cookies, and muffins that I'd had delivered from the local bakery down the road.

I heard voices and the handle of the door to the boardroom jiggle, so I turned my attention back to my computer screen and went back to completing the booking for Denver. Once that was confirmed, I proceeded to book him a reservation at the closest steak house I could find. I'd just finalized that when the boardroom door opened and out walked the members of the IT department, each of the men scattering toward the elevator.

It was only a matter of moments before Spencer came walking out of the room. He had already removed his tie, and his dress shirt was open at the collar. He appeared tense and on edge, and I bit my bottom lip as he met my eyes. He said nothing to me, so I quickly averted my eyes back down to the paperwork in front of me. Once he was inside his office, I looked up in time to see him place his paperwork on his desk.

I watched him as he stood at his desk, cell phone in hand, then reached for the phone on his desk. I couldn't help but admire him from afar; he was gorgeous. As my eyes climbed his body, he turned, our eyes meeting at the same time. Instead of smiling, he walked over to the door and kicked it closed. I jumped at the sound.

He'd asked me to stay, he'd said he wanted to talk to me, yet he hadn't said a single word. I'd been fielding calls from Brittany all afternoon, so no doubt he was in there calling her right now. Spencer rarely spoke of his ex to me; it wasn't my business, but I knew that suddenly there had been a lot of tension between the two of them. I decided that I wasn't waiting.

I began closing down all the programs I had opened, and then shut my monitor off. Anything he wanted to speak to me about could wait until tomorrow, I thought. If not, he could text me.

I'd just come back from the ladies room and was putting on my coat when the phone rang on my desk. I glanced to his closed door, then to the phone, and decided I'd better answer it.

"Finding Forever, Spencer Brooks office, Ainsley speaking."

"Ains, it's Dad."

"Oh...Hey, Dad," I said, glancing to Spencer's door again.

"Ains, did you forget we had plans tonight? The ballgame, pizza, and wings?"

I blew out a breath and turned away to look out the window. My father had been begging me to spend time with him. Since I'd begun working for Spencer, I'd had a lot of late work nights. "No, Dad, I didn't forget. Spencer was in meetings all day, and my desk looked like a bomb went off," I lied as I looked out over the city.

"Ainsley, how many more late nights are you going to be putting in? I think this is a tad ridiculous, don't you?"

I turned around to see Spencer leaning up against the doorframe, his eyes skimming my body before they met mine.

It's my dad, I mouthed to Spencer. He hung his head, and I could see his chest rising and falling in a silent chuckle.

"I'm not sure, Dad. I'm just trying to do a good job."

"What time do you figure you'll be home tonight?"

I looked to Spencer and tapped the face of my watch. He smiled, thought for a minute, and then mouthed ten.

"Ah I should be done about ten," I replied.

"All right." My father huffed his disappointment. "Drive careful."

"I will. Love you." I placed the phone into the receiver and looked over to Spencer. I could barely take my eyes off him, he looked so deliciously sexy.

"He wants you home, doesn't he," Spencer questioned and looked to the floor.

I nodded. "Honestly, it was my fault. I agreed to watch the game with him tonight. I should have known better."

"Were you getting ready to leave?" Spencer asked, looking around at the items on my desk.

I'd closed my notebook and had arranged all the items for tomorrow morning.

"I was. I figured maybe you needed some time, perhaps to speak with Brittany. She's been calling all day," I said, holding up the stack of messages she'd left. "Besides, you've had a long day."

"Brittany can wait, and yes, I have had a long day, but I wanted to run something by you before you go. Why don't you come on in for a few minutes."

I could see the want flash in his eyes as he looked at me, waiting for my answer. It was only a matter of minutes before I stood in Spencer's office. He sat behind his computer, tapping his fingers on the keyboard. He stopped, looked up at me, and blew out a breath.

"I see you booked the room as I asked."

I nodded and smiled. "And the restaurant. It's only a couple of blocks from the hotel. I figured it was the most logical choice. It looks amazing, and I figured with it being so close, you wouldn't have to take a cab, you could walk."

Spencer nodded, his face serious. "Perfect."

"Spencer, is everything okay?" I couldn't help but feel that there was a note of unnecessary tension between the two of us. "You looked...stressed." It was the only word I had for the look on his face and the tension I could see in his shoulders.

Spencer looked at me, then got up from his chair and walked around the desk. He slid in front of me and leaned against his desk, then pulled me into his arms and against his chest. "I am. It's just been...a day. I'm glad you stayed," he murmured, meeting my lips with a tender kiss.

I placed my arms on his shoulders. "You asked, and since I'm new, I can't exactly go doing whatever I want now can I. I mean...the boss...he would get mad...perhaps punish me."

I felt Spencer's chest rise and fall in laughter, a little bit of tension falling from his face. "Perhaps you are right," he said, holding me tighter against him. "But not tonight. Tonight, I just want to take you."

"You want to take me where?" I questioned, completely missing what he'd truly said.

His eyes met mine. I could feel the heat rise in my body, my cheeks growing warmer the longer he looked at me. He placed his fingers below my chin, bringing my mouth to his, and he bent down and kissed me hard, backing me up and pressing me against the wall.

I gripped his shirt as his tongue assaulted my mouth, his hands roaming my body. He gripped the bottom of my sweater and swiftly lifted it up and over my head, discarding it to the ground. I pulled at his shirt, ripping it from his pants, then reached for his belt, quickly loosening the buckle as he kissed me harder and with more want than I'd ever felt.

His lips left mine as he knelt down in front of me. He placed a gentle kiss on stomach and looked up at me. I ran my fingers through his hair as he gently tugged at my skirt, pulling it down over my hips. I stood there in my matching bra and panties and was surprised when he buried his face between my legs.

I let out a moan when I felt the pressure of his tongue through my panties. I fisted his hair as he continued. I jumped at a sound out in the hall and placed my hand on his shoulder. "Spencer, there's someone..." I whispered, fighting to hold back my moan.

"It's the cleaning crew. You'll have to be quiet. I don't

plan on stopping," he whispered as he began running his tongue over my panties again, teasing me with every lick.

"Spencer, they are right outside the door," I whispered breathlessly as he continued torturing me with his tongue.

"Door is shut, they won't come in. They know that rule well."

He didn't stop. Instead, he pushed my panties to the side and buried his tongue in me, licking and sucking. My breathing quickened and my legs began to shake so bad I could barely keep myself up. I slid my fingers into his hair, grasping as I tilted my head back against the wall, looking toward the ceiling, and bit my bottom lip fighting to keep quiet.

"Give me your leg," he gritted, and he grasped my calf, lifting my left leg over his shoulder, opening me up to him. It was all I could do to keep from screaming out as he slid two fingers inside of me and continued this mind-blowing form of torture with his tongue.

In a matter of seconds, I could feel wave after wave of pleasure beginning to run through my body. I gripped at the wall as my orgasm ripped through me as Spencer relentlessly lapped and sucked at my center. I brought my hand up to my mouth and bit the back of it to stifle my cries. My entire body went limp as I rested against the wall, breathing hard and fast.

Spencer kissed his way up my body, pulling me against

him. "Come away with me, Ainsley. To Denver," he whispered.

Without even realizing what it was I was agreeing to, I nodded my head, my eyes closed as I tried to regain the part of myself I'd just lost. It was then I felt Spencer grip my arms, spin me around, and press me flat down onto his desk. I was still breathing hard as he sank his large, hot, throbbing cock into me, pumping hard.

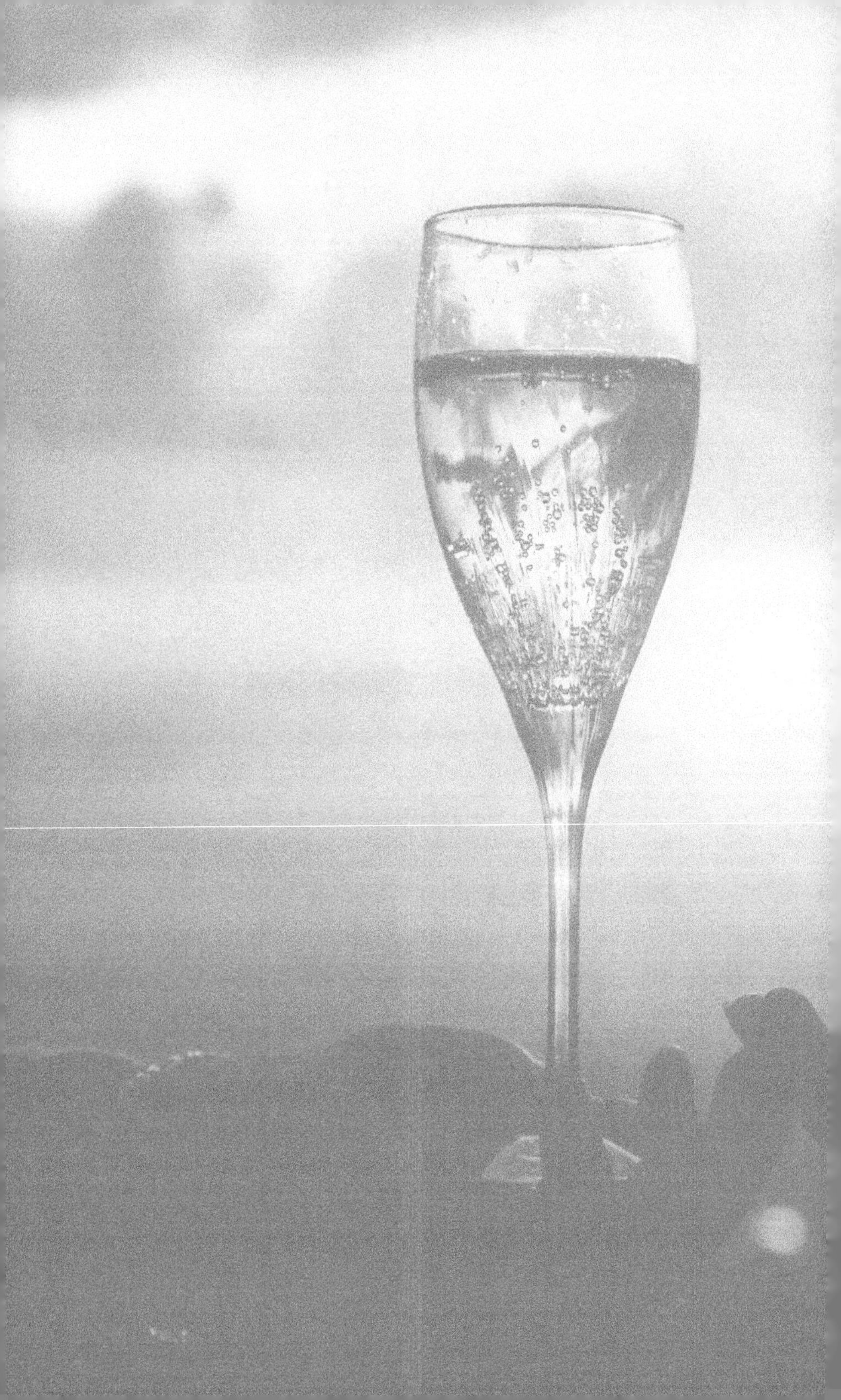

Spencer

RomanticAlpha42: You just about ready to head out?

I closed the trunk of my car and leaned up against it. This was the third time I'd messaged Ainsley in the past hour, and I still didn't have a response from her.

I knew that Jon had been giving her a hard time over the last couple of weeks for working so much. She'd repeatedly told him that she was just trying her hardest to impress me enough for her to keep her job, but Jon wouldn't listen. He'd finally called me the other day and asked me not to keep her at the office so late, and I'd done as I'd been asked.

I ran back into the house to grab my laptop bag and

felt my phone vibrate in my pocket. I quickly pulled it out and looked down at the message that sat on my screen.

BabyGirl89: Dad's pissed. Perhaps I shouldn't go.

I blew out a breath, picked up my laptop, and made my way out to the car where I placed it into the trunk and shut it. This was something I'd been anticipating; it was also something that I wasn't going to let happen. She was coming with me. I pocketed my phone and made my way over to Ainsley's.

I knocked on the door and waited, listening as Jon yelled from inside. I was about to knock again when the door was pulled open, and Jon stood there looking out at me with irritation.

"Spencer!"

"Hey, Jon, I just came by to pick up Ainsley."

Ainsley had shared with me numerous times over the last few nights how uneasy she felt about us going away together. She was afraid that her father suspected something was going on between us, but I assured her he didn't.

"We have a flight to catch at three," I said, looking down at my watch. "Is she ready?"

I could see the tension in Jon's jaw as he opened the door and stepped aside to let me in.

"Ainsley..." Jon yelled.

"Anything wrong?" I questioned. "You seem...tense."

"She's hiding something from me. She's been acting funny for the past few weeks. It's not like her not to talk to me, but no matter how much I ask, she just gets more closed off," Jon said, looking in the direction of Ainsley's room.

"Perhaps you're pushing too hard."

"I think I know my daughter," Jon gritted. "She's hiding something, I know it. I just hope it isn't drugs. Her mother got involved in drugs. It didn't end well for her."

I looked to the floor. Jon was a mess. "I can assure you it's not drugs. She hasn't missed work, Jon. She's very on the ball with everything. She isn't even late coming back from lunch, and I have seen no signs of alcohol abuse. Perhaps it's a woman's issue," I suggested.

Just then I heard a door open, and Ainsley stepped into the living room carrying a bag over her shoulder and her purse on the other. "Sorry, I'm ready."

I glanced at both bags and cleared my throat. "You have your laptop, right?"

Ainsley met my eyes, a look of unease on her face as she shook her head. "Oh gosh, how could I forget that." She laughed nervously as she dropped her bags and headed back down to her bedroom.

I looked to Jon, who squinted in Ainsley's direction. "See what I mean?" Jon said, looking at me. "Business trip and she forgets her computer. She's been like this for weeks."

"In her defense, Jon, I almost forgot mine." I chuckled. "Give her a break. This is her first real job, and her first work-related trip. Surely, it's just nerves," I said, trying to cover for her. "She's very eager to impress."

"What's just nerves?" Ainsley said, stepping back into the living room, her laptop bag slung over her shoulder.

"Why you're acting so strange," I said, trying to hint at her to gather herself as I bent down and picked up her bags. "We've got to get going," I said, glancing at my watch.

"I'll see you Monday, Dad," Ainsley said, then leaned in to give him a hug. She stepped out onto the porch first, then I followed her, waiting until she was down the stairs, and then we proceeded to make our way to my car.

"See you later. See you, Spencer. I'll keep an eye on your house. What time do you think you'll be back on Monday?"

Ainsley continued walking, but I turned. "Our flight lands at nine in the morning. We will head to the office from the airport, so I will say dinnertime."

"Sounds good." Jon called out, "Love you, Ains."

Ainsley lifted her arm, waving good-bye, then she stopped outside of my car. I loaded her things into the trunk, and then together we climbed into the car. Once inside, I started the engine and backed out of the driveway, leaving our houses behind.

"Thank you for coming over. I couldn't take it. Seriously, I was about to cancel."

"Understandable. What was going on?"

"He just keeps telling me that I am acting strange. I've done nothing. I get up, I go to work, I call if I'm going to be late. Last night, however, he was all over me about it."

"He asked me the other day to stop working you so much. I of course told him I would, and then you probably went home and told him about this weekend." I chuckled.

"Yeah, he wasn't too thrilled about it, that much I can say."

I could see the stress all over Ainsley's face. I reached over and placed my hand on her thigh. "It's going to be okay, Ains."

She met my eyes, then looked down at my hand, her small hand coming down and resting on top of mine.

I'd signed the papers for the new office space and sent a message to Ainsley asking her to begin listing job openings within the company directory while I waited for the cab.

Seconds later, I looked down to my phone to see a message from BabyGirl89. A smile landed on my lips as I opened it.

BabyGirl89: Congratulations! I'll have a surprise for you once you return, to celebrate.

I was standing on the sidewalk grinning like an idiot when my phone began to ring. Expecting it to be Ainsley, I didn't wait for the call display to populate before I answered it.

"So, Ains...I can't wait to see what you have in mind for my surprise."

"Spencer? What are you talking about?" Brittany's voice sounded in my ear.

The second I heard her voice, my body stiffened. "Brittany..."

"Yes, where the hell are you? I tried calling the house all weekend, but there was no answer."

"I'm in Denver, acquiring new office space. Not that you care."

"I see, and Ainsley's with you?"

"She's my assistant, Brittany. Of course, she is here with me," I bit out.

"Uh huh."

I rolled my eyes. "What is it you needed?" I questioned, just wanting to get rid of her.

"Spencer, I'd expect you to have a better assistant, honestly. I've been leaving messages for you at the office and you've never called me back. Has she been giving them to you?"

I blew out a breath. "Yes, Brittany, she has given them to me. I've been busy, and you never said it was an emergency. I planned to call you tomorrow when I get back into the office."

"Well how on earth would you know if it was an emergency or not. You never called me back."

"I'd assume that if it was an emergency that you would say that. Can you please just tell me what it is you want?"

"Why? Do you need to run off to Miss Twenty-Year-Old?"

"Brittany, what exactly are you insinuating?"

"I'm sure you can put two and two together, Spencer. Honestly."

The tone of her voice made me want to punch the brick wall I stood against. She wasn't being fair. Although it shouldn't have surprised me; she never was fair. She hadn't been fair during our separation or our divorce.

"If you must know, I am having dinner with a couple of clients. If it makes you feel better, Ainsley is not joining us. Now, if you'd like to tell me what it is you need..."

"Fine, Spencer, I am wondering if we can switch weekends with Nikki. Something has come up on my weekend."

"So, hire a sitter, Brittany. You know I have planned out every weekend I have with her. If you can't get a sitter, she can of course come and stay with me, but I'm not switching."

"It's just like you to be difficult. Shall I call the lawyer?" she threatened.

This was just like Brittany. Whenever she didn't get her way, she threatened me with legal action. I blew out a breath. "No need to get the lawyer involved. We can switch."

"Thank you. Now you aren't going to leave her with Ainsley are you? I mean, she did tell me you left her Valentine's weekend."

I rolled my eyes and looked up to the sky, then noticed the cab pull up to the sidewalk. "You knew that I had a prior engagement that weekend. It was a work-related event, and in case I need to remind you, it is the way I pay for child support, so yes, Ainsley stayed with Nikki."

"I will have to let the lawyer know that too."

I could feel the anger surge through my body. I could never win with her. "Listen, I have to go, my cab is here. I will call you tomorrow."

"Fine, Spencer."

I hung up the phone and opened the cab door and climbed in. The second the door shut, the cab driver pulled away from the curb and sped off toward the hotel.

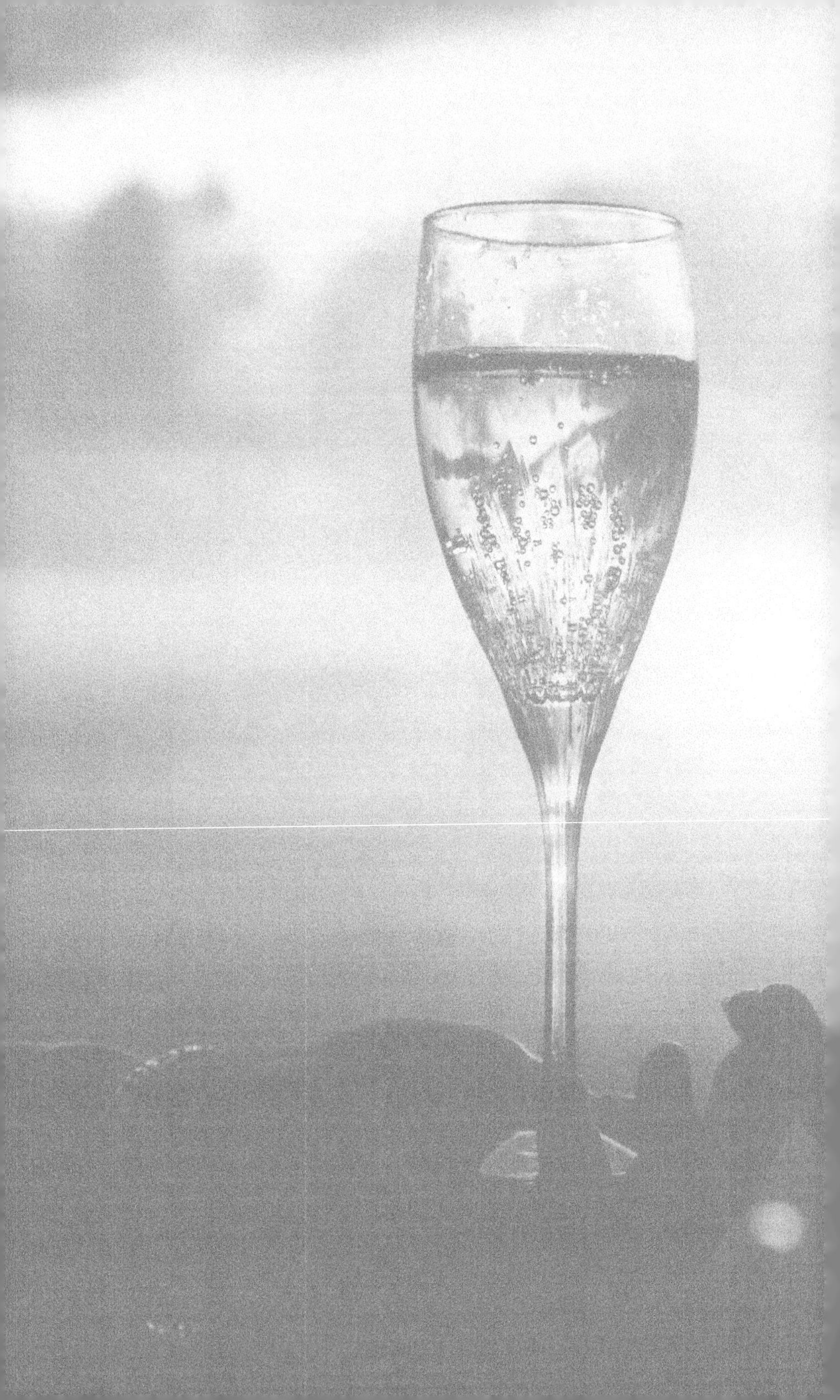

Ainsley

"What time do we fly?" I questioned, yawning, looking over to Spencer. He stared at the screen of his laptop, looking over the job postings I'd created. He studied them, a slight scowl on his face. "Seven," he bit out.

"So we have to be at the airport at what, three?" I asked, looking to the clock on the side table.

"Close to it," he mumbled.

I rolled back over onto my side and stared at the wall. When I had talked to Spencer at the end of his meeting with the realtor he'd been in a great mood. It had taken him longer than he expected to return. I didn't think anything of it until dinner. He was mostly silent, very distant, and closed off all the way through dinner, which had me worried.

We'd walked back to the hotel in silence, my arm laced through his. When we stepped inside the lobby, we could hear piano music coming from the lounge over. Spencer looked at me, then leaned into my ear. "Ainsley, do you mind if I take an hour, get a drink?"

His eyes were full of a sadness I'd never seen before. I simply nodded my head, raised up onto my toes, and placed a small, tender kiss on his lips. "Sure, Spencer, go ahead. I'll be upstairs."

"Thank you," he said, kissing my forehead.

I watched as he walked over to the lounge and entered. He took a seat just inside the door, and I stood there watching him for a few minutes. He pulled at the knot in his tie, then removed it, placing it on the table in front of him. Then he unbuttoned the top of his shirt, ran his fingers through his hair, and relaxed back in his chair. Perhaps the meeting hadn't gone well, and he hadn't wanted to say anything, I thought to myself. Whatever was bothering him was none of my business. I walked over to the elevator bank and hit the call button.

Once I was back in the room, I'd decided to have a hot bath. I filled the jacuzzi with hot water and a little bubble bath and climbed in, allowing the heat to sink into my muscles.

I kept an eye on the clock, and once I'd climbed out of the tub, I reached for the box that contained the gift Spencer had given me when we arrived. I lifted the lid and looked down at the prettiest lacey red-and-black teddy, remembering the way he'd growled in my ear how he couldn't wait to see me in it. I picked up the lacey material and held it up in front of me. Tonight, I would give him his wish.

Once I had gotten it on I glanced to the clock, I knew he'd be coming back any moment, so I sprawled across the bed. I'd just gotten comfortable, and like clockwork, I heard the click of the door. Except his reaction hadn't been what I'd expected.

He'd walked in, threw his tie down on the table, and walked right by me, mumbling something about needing to take a shower. He didn't even look my way; he just marched into the bathroom and shut the door behind him.

I rolled onto my back and stared up at the ceiling, my eyes burning. It had taken a lot for me to put myself out there like that, and he hadn't even noticed. I got up, slipped out of the teddy, folding it up neatly, and placed it into a secret pocket in my suitcase. Then I slipped into my usual T-shirt and shorts and crawled under the covers.

His response, or lack of, had been bothering me all night. After his shower, he'd grabbed his laptop and climbed into bed and buried himself in work, checking over all the listings I'd done. It was almost eleven. I never expected he'd still be working on them this late.

"Spencer, it's almost eleven."

"Yep, almost finished. If the light is bothering, you I can move to the desk. That way you can turn the lights off," he mumbled.

I blew out a breath, not saying anything, and rolled onto my back. "Is something wrong, Spencer?"

"No, why do you ask?"

I swallowed back the tears that threatened to fall. "You've been very distant. All through dinner, the walk back, you barely said anything. Then when you came back here you didn't even notice...." My throat burned, and I had to stop talking for fear I started crying.

"Didn't notice what?" he questioned, tearing his eyes away from the laptop for the first time in hours and looked down at me.

"Nothing, it's nothing," I said, swallowing hard, turning away from him.

I listened as I fought back tears. I heard the lid of laptop shut, felt the bed move, then the light was turned off and we were bathed in the light from the TV. I felt him slide his arm around my waist, the other move under my pillow as he gathered me in his arms.

"What didn't I notice?" he whispered.

When I didn't answer him right away, he placed a kiss on the side of my neck and pulled my body into his. I lay in his arms, trying to fight back tears as he tried to comfort me for an unknown reason.

We lay in silence for a few moments, then he cleared his throat. "I'm sorry I've been distant. Brittany called me before I arrived back here this afternoon. She wanted me to switch her weekends for Nikki. When I refused, she threatened me with a lawyer, like she always does. Then she started going on about you. Apparently, she must have a bit of a jealous streak in her. She doesn't seem to like you very much, and I guess you could say it threw me a bit."

I knew exactly how she could be. When she'd called for Spencer at the office, she'd passed some remarks my way that I hadn't appreciated. I hadn't told Spencer because I knew it would make him angry. I'd just taken her messages and passed them on like a good assistant would. Besides, it wasn't my place to talk to him about his ex.

"I'm sorry, Spencer."

"She said some things that rubbed me the wrong way. I guess you could say it took away all my focus."

"Were they things about me?" I questioned. I needed to know if she had bashed me to him.

"Why do you ask that?" Spencer frowned.

"No reason."

"Ainsley, has she said things to you?"

I swallowed hard, but the tears burned the corners of my eyes. I bit my bottom lip and nodded. "She's brutal," I cried. "At first, I barely paid attention to the things she'd said, but after the fifth call the other day, I couldn't anymore. Does she know about us?"

"No, Ainsley, she doesn't. She will try to convince you otherwise. She's a manipulator, and she will work to find out the information she wants, especially when she suspects something, but I swear to you, I haven't said a word."

I wiped at my eyes and nodded my head, then rolled onto my back to look up at Spencer. He studied me for a moment, then leaned down and took my mouth with his. I could already feel his growing arousal as he pulled me into him, allowing me to rest my head on his shoulder.

"I don't want you to worry about it, okay? I also want you to tell me when she gets out of line next time so I can stop it."

I looked at Spencer, not saying anything.

"Promise me, Ainsley."

I nodded my head. "I promise."

He shut the TV off and we lay in the dark in silence for a few moments. He cleared his throat. "So are you going to tell me what it was I missed?"

I bit my bottom lip, thankful he couldn't see how red my face was. "Maybe another time," I whispered.

I relaxed into his side, my head on his chest, the warmth of his body comforting me. I knew that come tomorrow night I would miss this, miss falling asleep in his arms, and because of that I didn't want the night to end. I rolled away from him, and I felt him roll onto his side, pulling me back against his chest. I closed my eyes, relishing in the warmth of his body, and felt his lips on the back of my neck, his breath tickling me. "I'm going to miss this tomorrow night," he whispered. "So much."

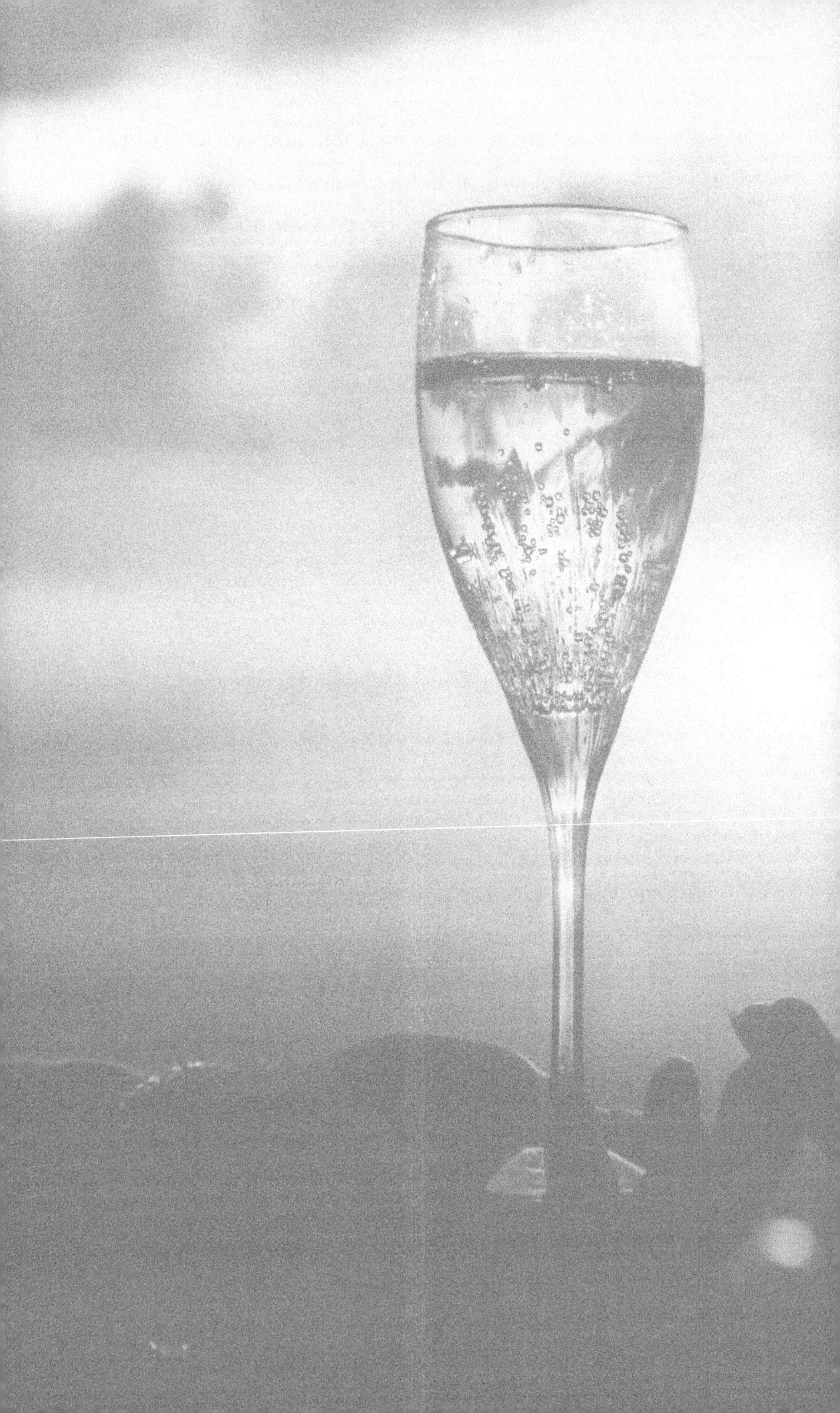

Spencer

The trip home had been a long one. Ainsley and I had returned a little after ten. From the airport we'd gone to the office, and while I spent most of my day in meetings with human resources going over the hiring for the new office, Ainsley worked away on some monthly reports for me.

When I'd returned from the meetings, I'd noticed Ainsley looked exhausted as she worked away. I'd gone into my office and gathered my things and then made my way over to her desk. She looked up at me from behind her computer screen and gave me a soft smile.

"I'm just about finished with those reports you'd asked for, except for two. I think I am going to need a little more time on those."

I didn't say anything. I just studied her gorgeous face and nodded.

"I mean, I can get them done for you before I go, but it may take me until eight."

I looked down the hall to the left, then to the right, before taking a step in behind her desk and placing my hands on her shoulders. I gently began massaging her and could feel her body stiffen at my touch. I bent down and placed a kiss on top of her head then leaned in and whispered into her ear, "No more work tonight. It's a good night to head home and get some rest."

She looked up at me, then smiled, placing her right hand onto mine. "You're right," she murmured. "This can wait until tomorrow then?"

"It can."

I reached in front of her and shut off her computer screen, then held my hand out for her to take. She hesitantly took it then stood up and reached for her purse and coat. It was only a matter of minutes before we were speeding off in my car.

I'd been home for a little over three hours. I'd eaten and showered and now stood in the kitchen in boxers and a T-shirt and reached for my favorite rock glass from the cupboard. I placed it onto the counter and listened as the ice I dropped into the glass jingled. I reached for my favorite bottle of scotch and poured myself three fingers, then I grabbed the remote and turned on the radio, jazz pouring out of the speaker.

This was my quiet time, the time I usually relished having, only tonight something felt different. I sat down and closed my eyes and thought about the kiss she'd given me before I'd shut the trunk of the car. The trunk had given us just enough privacy to keep her father from seeing anything out of his front window. That kiss had been soft, gentle, and firm, and one she had initiated herself for the first time. Then she took her bags and made her way home, while I watched.

I'd regretted not noticing her last night when she'd put herself out there. I'd known that had taken a lot for her to do. I'd walked in like an asshole, not even looking her way, completely consumed with the fact that my ex-wife was once again holding Nikki over my head. Even though I'd talked to her about it, it still was haunting me.

I blew out a breath, took a sip of my scotch, and then sat down at the table and pulled my laptop in front of me. I had paperwork that needed to get finished, yet I couldn't concentrate. Instead, I glanced down at my phone, hoping that Ainsley would have messaged me, but there was nothing.

I took another sip of my scotch and rested my head against the back of my chair, closing my eyes, allowing the music to invade me. I jumped at the sound of my phone vibrating against the table and smiled as I looked down at my screen.

BabyGirl89: Are you busy??

RomanticAlpha42: It depends on what you consider busy.

I smiled to myself as I watched the three dots jump around on the screen. I picked up my glass and took a mouthful of scotch and almost choked as an image of Ainsley in the bra and panty set appeared before me. Instantly, my cock hardened, and I very much wished I'd turned my attention to her our last night away.

RomanticAlpha42: Are you trying to kill me.

BabyGirl89: Not my intention ;)

RomanticAlpha42: What exactly is your intention?

BabyGirl89: I guess you could say that I'm feeling adventurous.

RomanticAlpha42: Feeling adventurous? I have an idea...my front door is open.

I watched as the three dots began jumping around, then went away, then began again, then went away for good. I left my phone on the table, adjusted my hard cock, and got up to pour another glass of scotch. I had a feeling I was going to need it. I set my glass down and plopped two ice cubes in the glass again, then heard someone clear their throat behind me.

I turned abruptly to find Ainsley, standing in the doorway of the room, leaning up against the doorframe. She wore her bathrobe, which now hung open just enough for me to catch a peak of her in the teddy I'd bought for her.

My eyes washed over her body. She looked good enough to eat. "My God, you look...."

"Tell me, tell me how I look," she said in a low, throaty growl as she grabbed the tie of her bathrobe and swung it around, her eyes giving off a playful glint.

I didn't wait. Instantly, I walked over to her, taking her in my arms as she wrapped her arms around my neck and met my mouth. I pushed her up against the wall, assaulting her mouth with my tongue as I pressed my body against hers. Then I lifted her up, wrapped her legs around my waist, and carried her down the hall to my bedroom, kicking the door shut behind me.

Note from the Author

Dear Readers,

Originally Our Little Secret was published in the Take Me to Bed Collection. I never planned to republish this story until I revisited this story. I added much more to the story than in it's original form and decided to go ahead and publish it. I'd like to thank you for taking the time to read Spencer and Ainsley's story. Spencer Brooks is one character I can't seem to get enough of, and you will be able to catch more of Ainsley and Spencer in Our Little Surprise coming in August. I can honestly say I don't think I am done with this couple yet and look forward to writing more about these characters.

If you loved Our Little Secret, please take a quick moment and drop me a review. If you loved Ainsley and

NOTE FROM THE AUTHOR

Spencer and want more, than be sure to preorder Our Little Surprise.

Much Love,
    S.L. Sterling

Coming Soon
Our Little Surprise – August 15th

The preorders from both of these books plus a percentage of the first months sales will be donated to Cope Service Dogs.

About the Author

S.L. Sterling had been an avid reader since she was a child, often found getting lost in books. Today if she isn't writing or plotting, she can be found buried in a romance novel with a cup of coffee at her side. S.L. Sterling lives with her husband and dogs in Northern Ontario.

Stay up to date with my Monthly Newsletter

Visit my Website

Join my Reader Group
Sterlings Silver Sapphires

Other Titles by S.L. Sterling

It Was Always You

On A Silent Night

Bad Company

Back to You this Christmas

Fireside Love

Holiday Wishes

Saviour Boy

The Boy Under the Gazebo

The Greatest Gift

Into the Sunset

The Malone Brother Series

A Kiss Beneath the Stars

In Your Arms

His to Hold

Finding Forever with You

Vegas MMA

Dagger

Doctors of Eastport General

Doctor Desire

All I Want for Christmas (Contemporary Romance Holiday Collection)

Constraint (KB Worlds: Everyday Heroes)

9 781989 566329